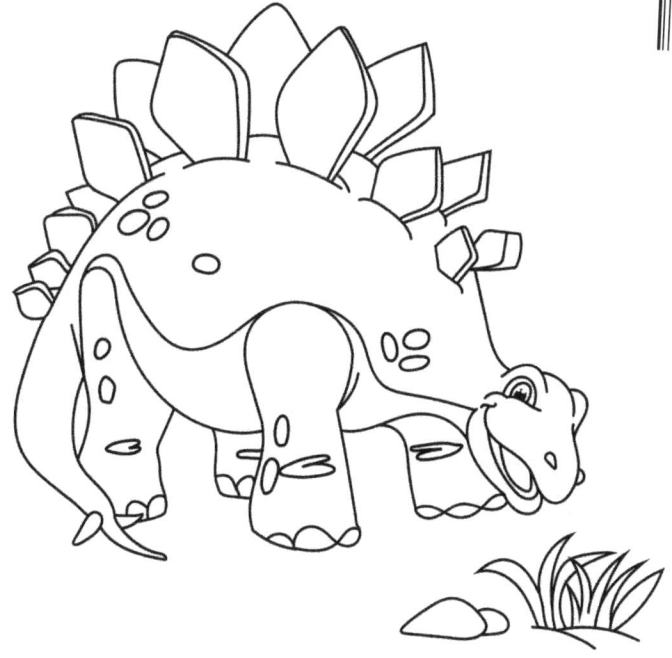

Dinosaur
Coloring Book for Kids

CREATIVE COLORING PRESS

Copyright © 2018 by DP Kids
All rights reserved. This book or any portion thereof
may not be reproduced or used in any manner whatsoever without the express
written permission of the publisher
except for the use of brief quotations in a book review.
First edition: 2018

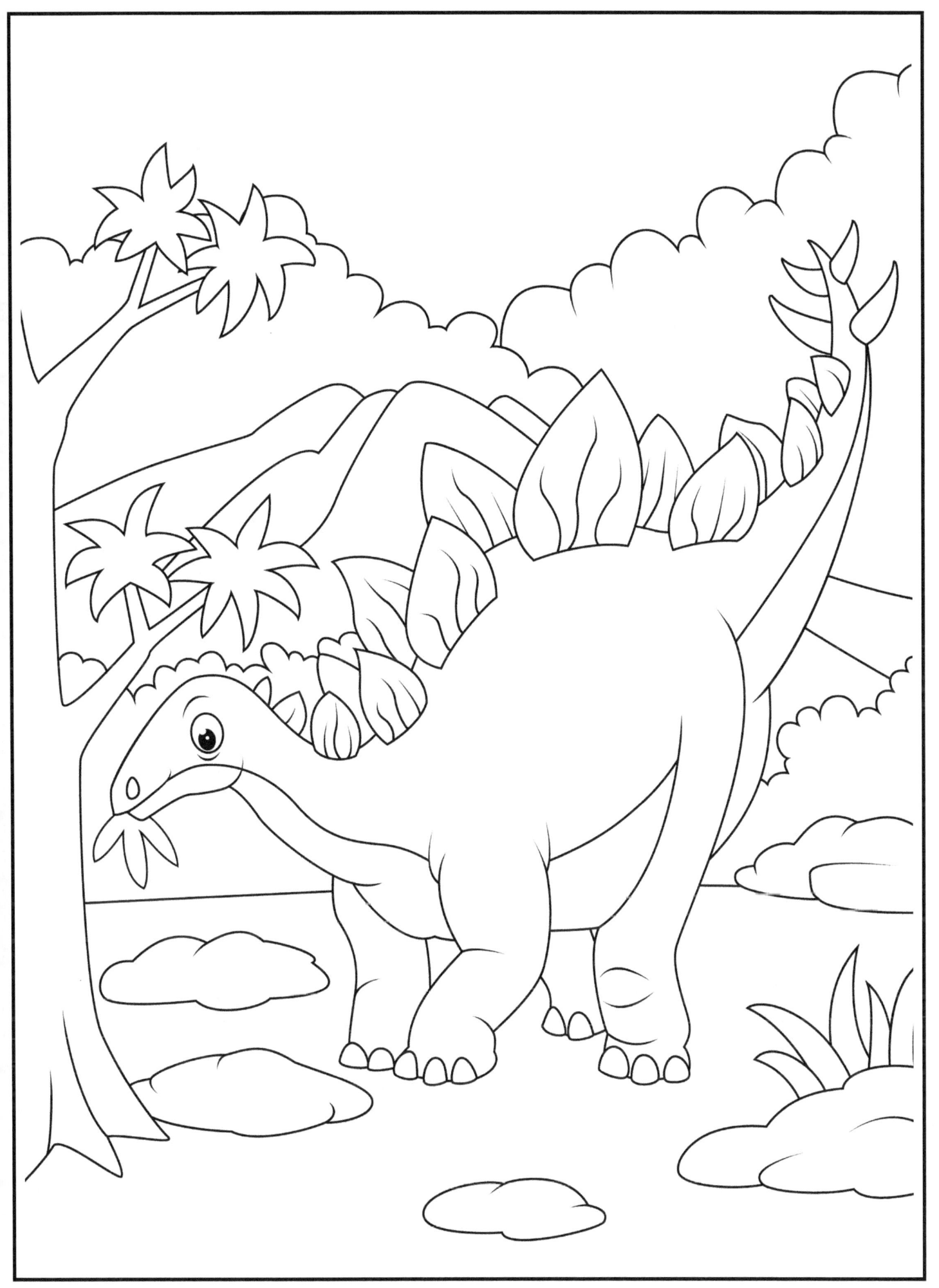

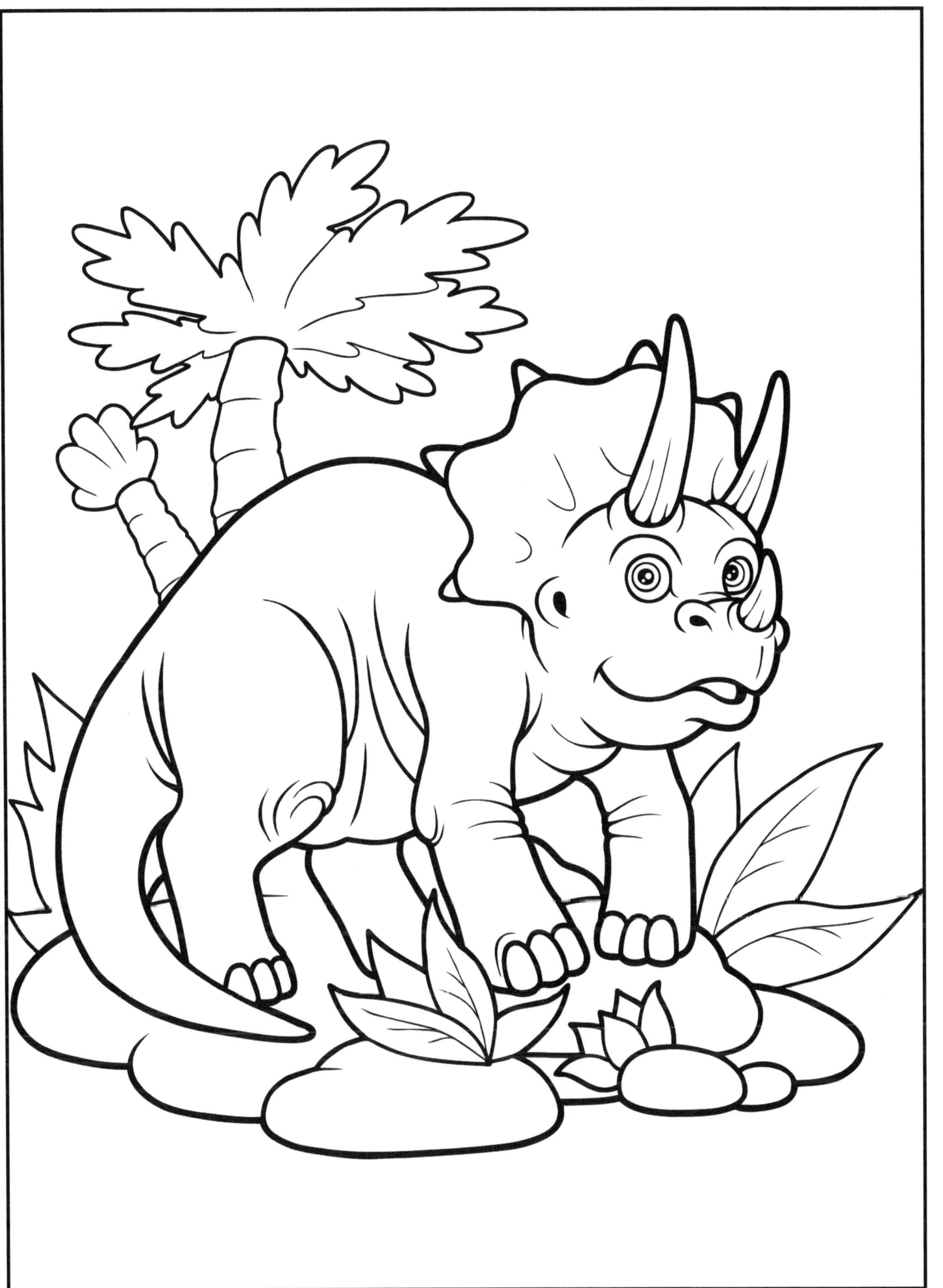

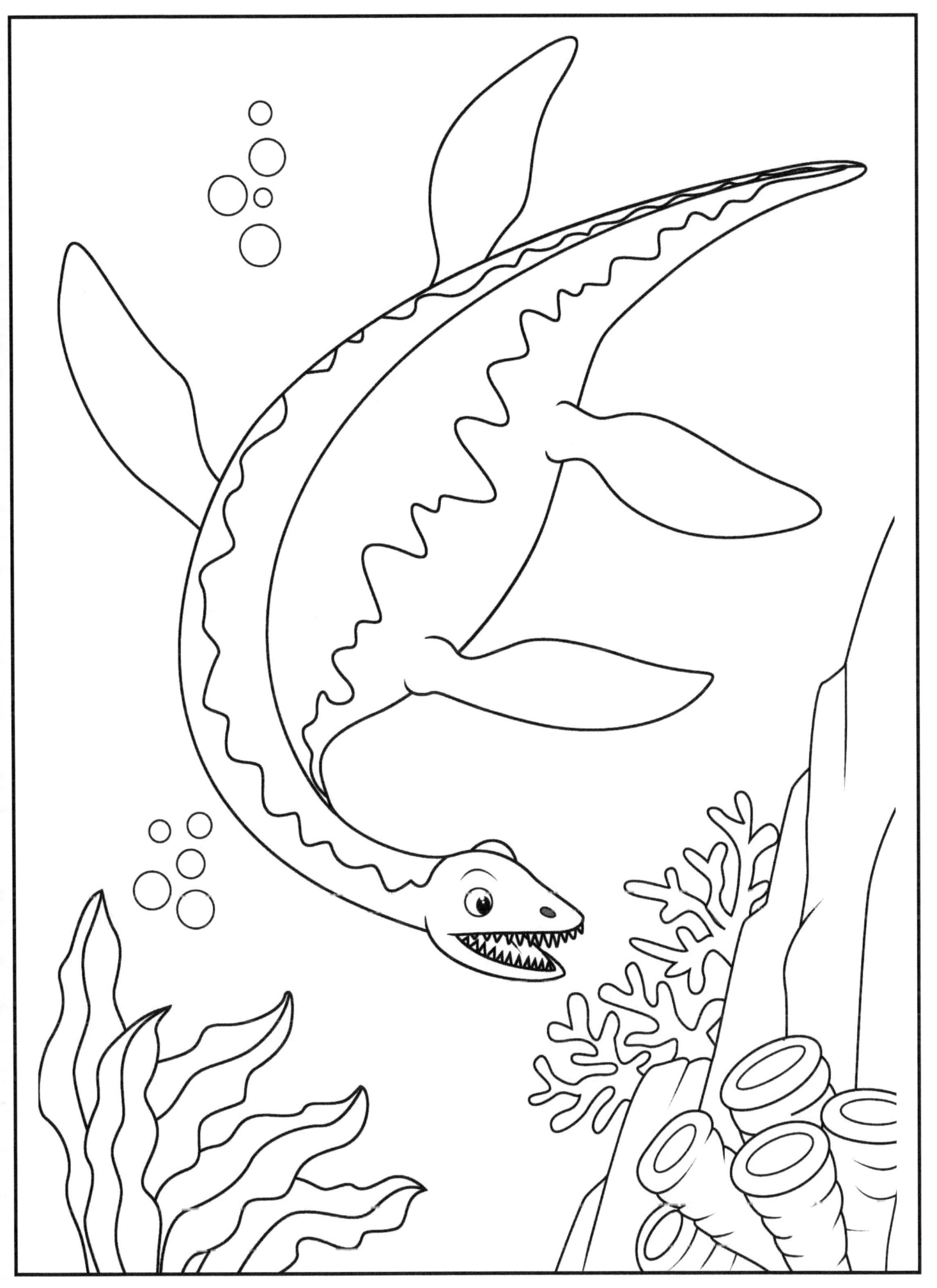

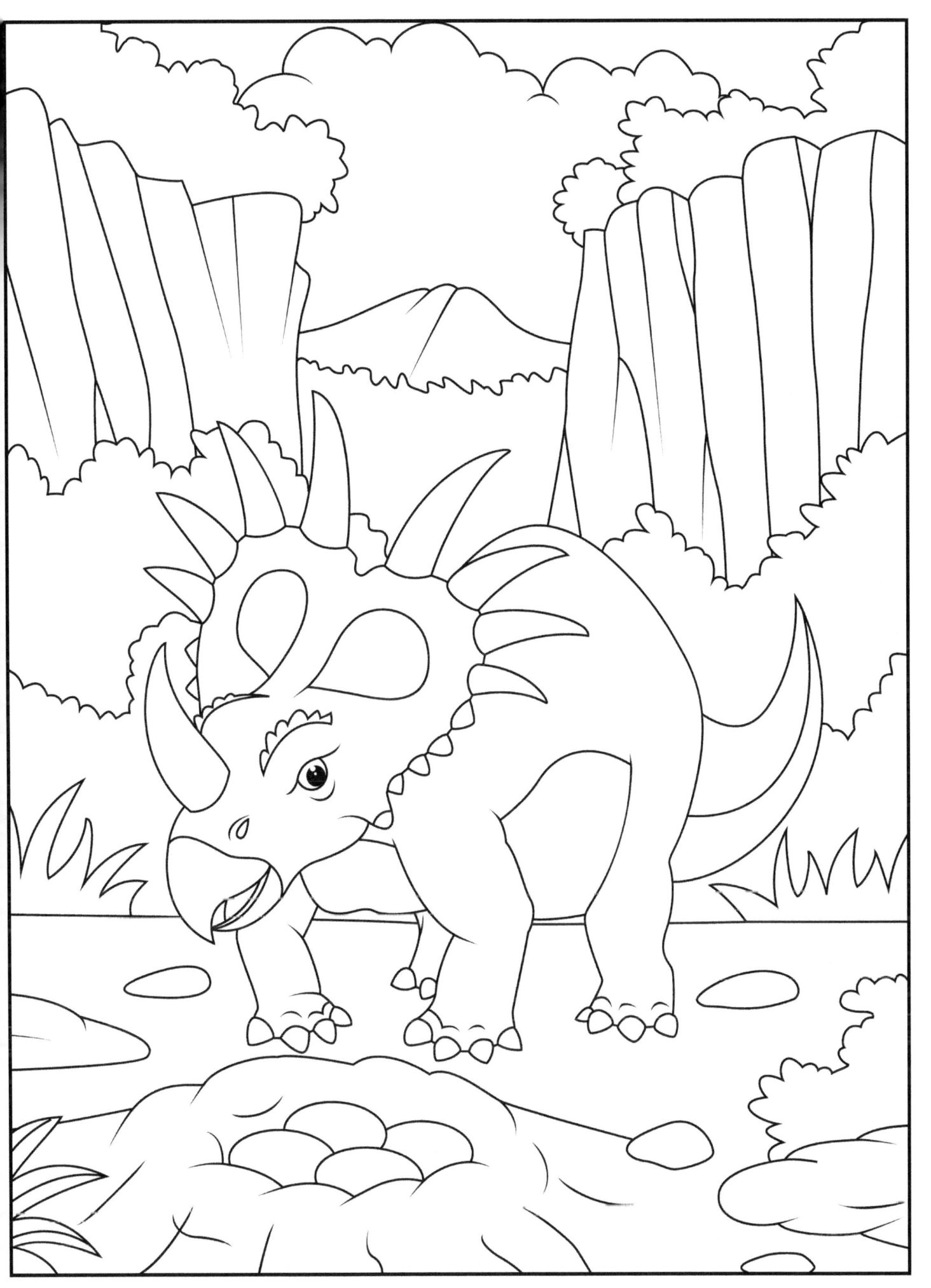

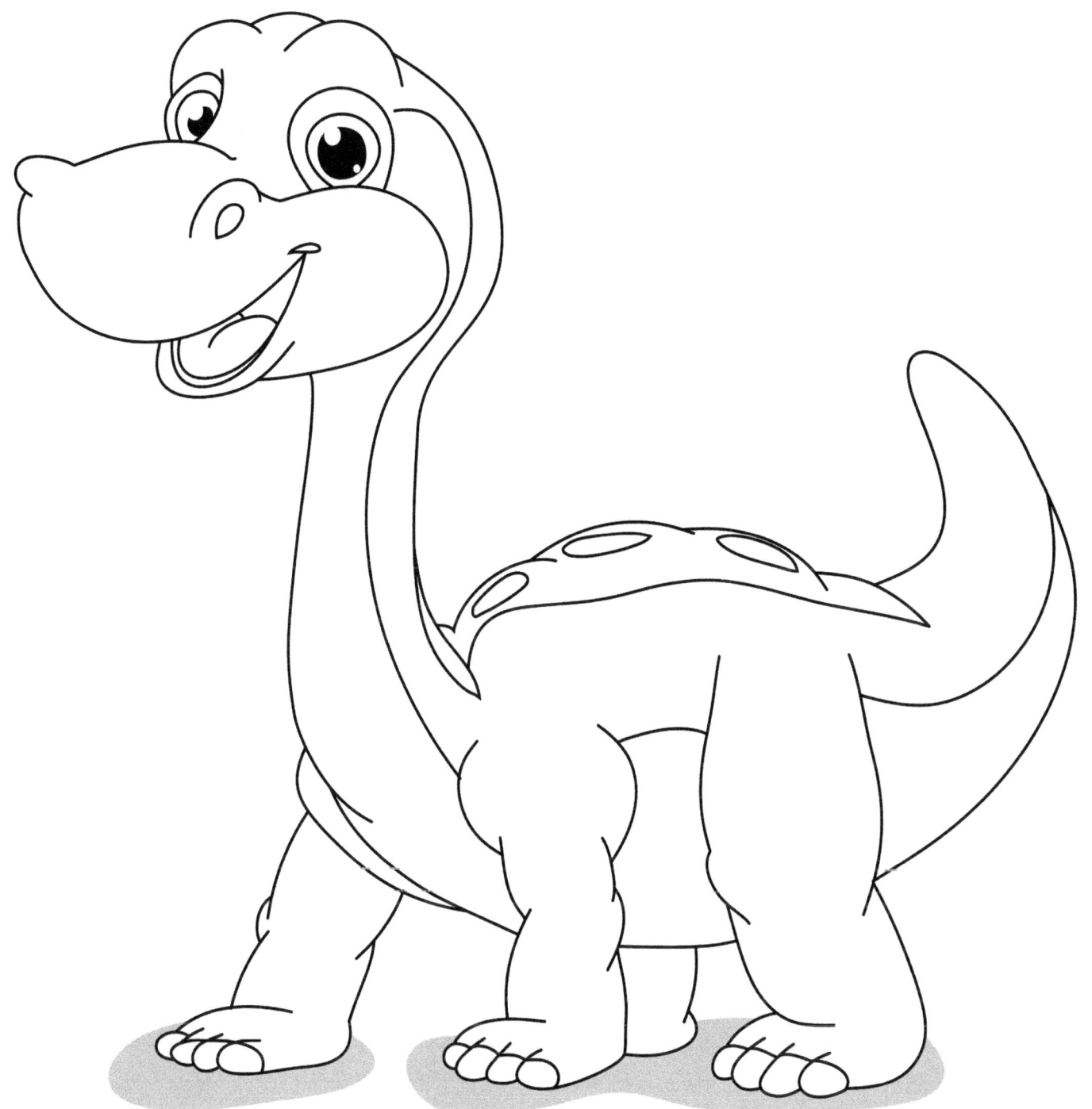

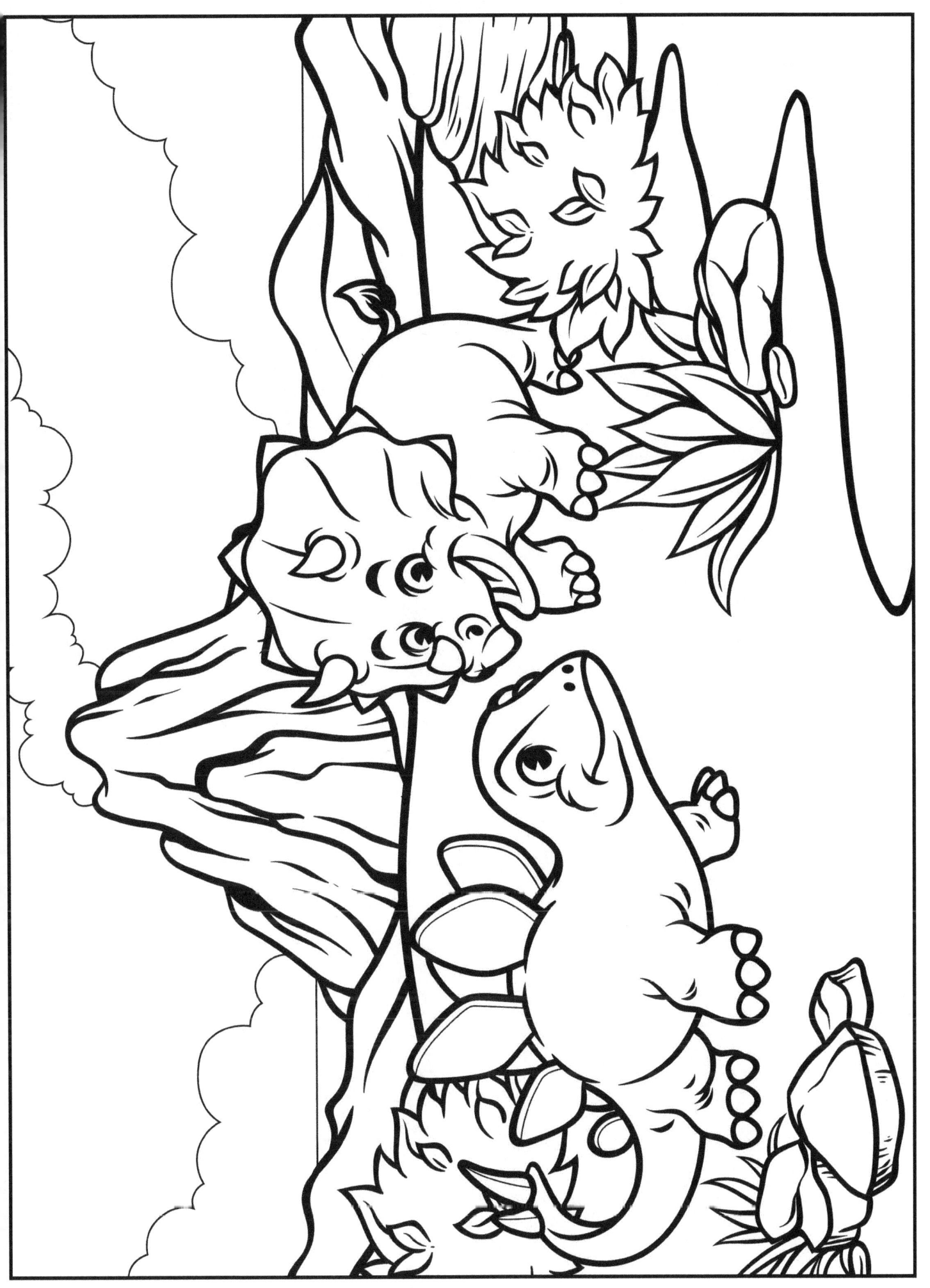

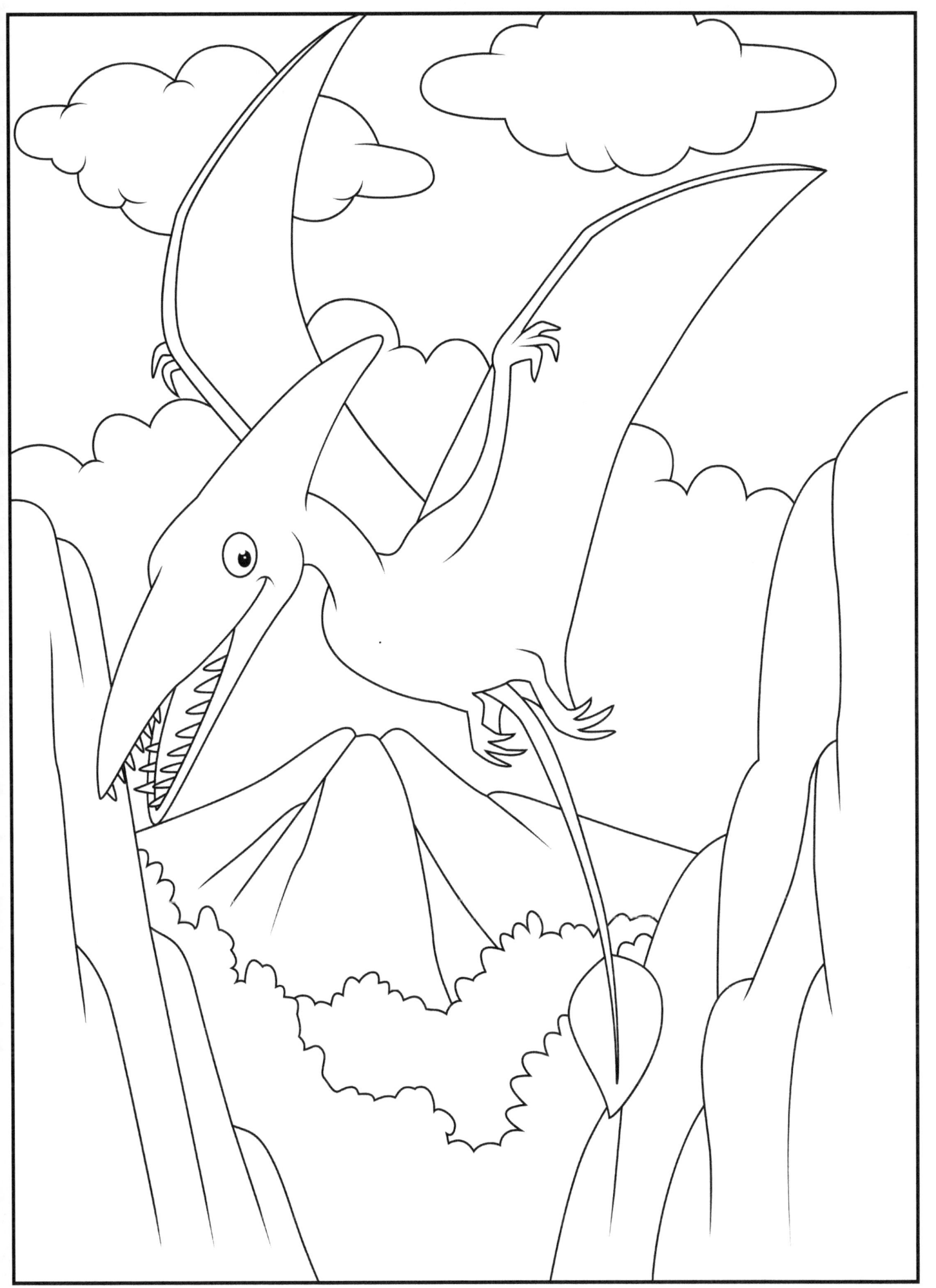

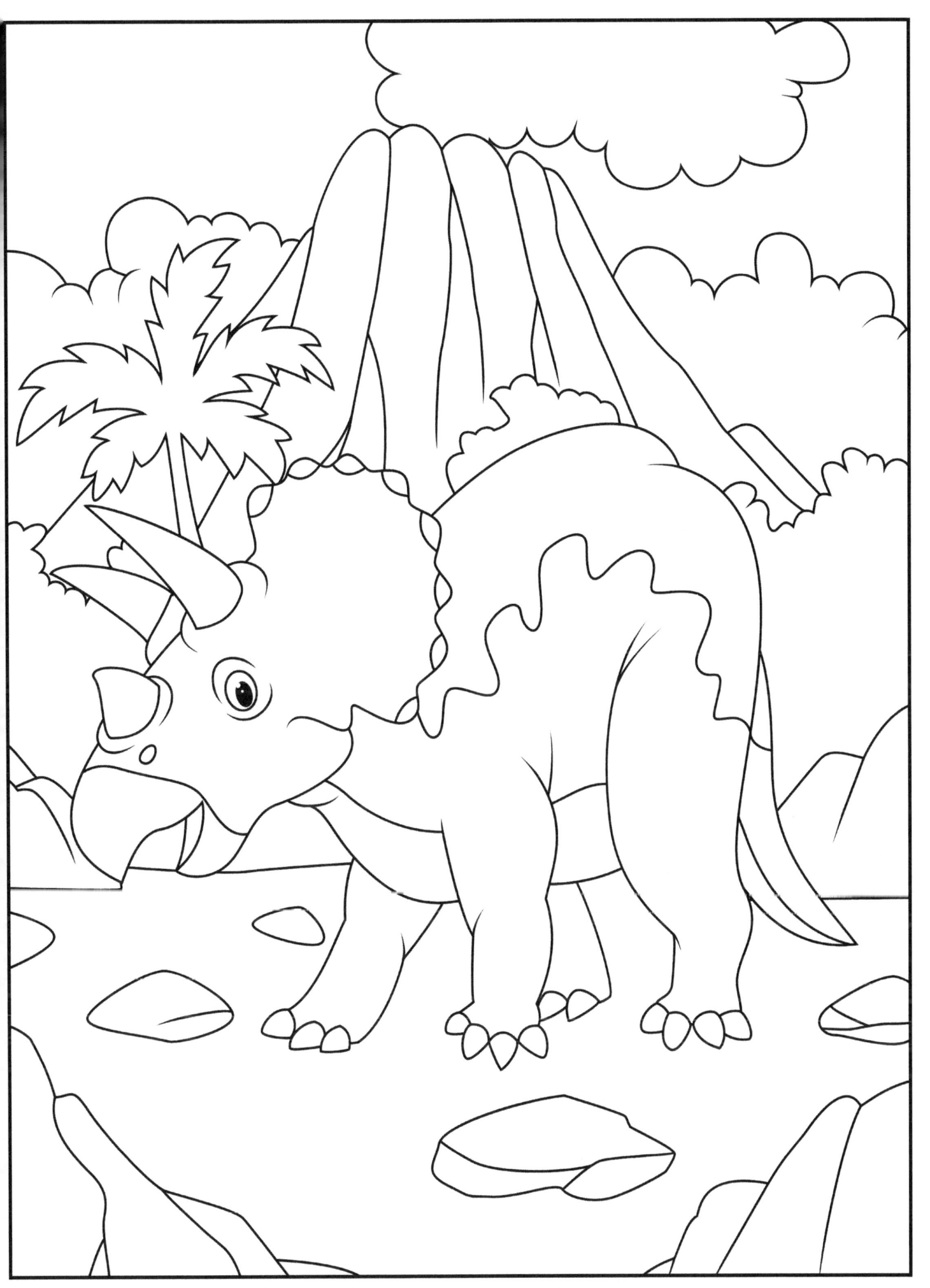

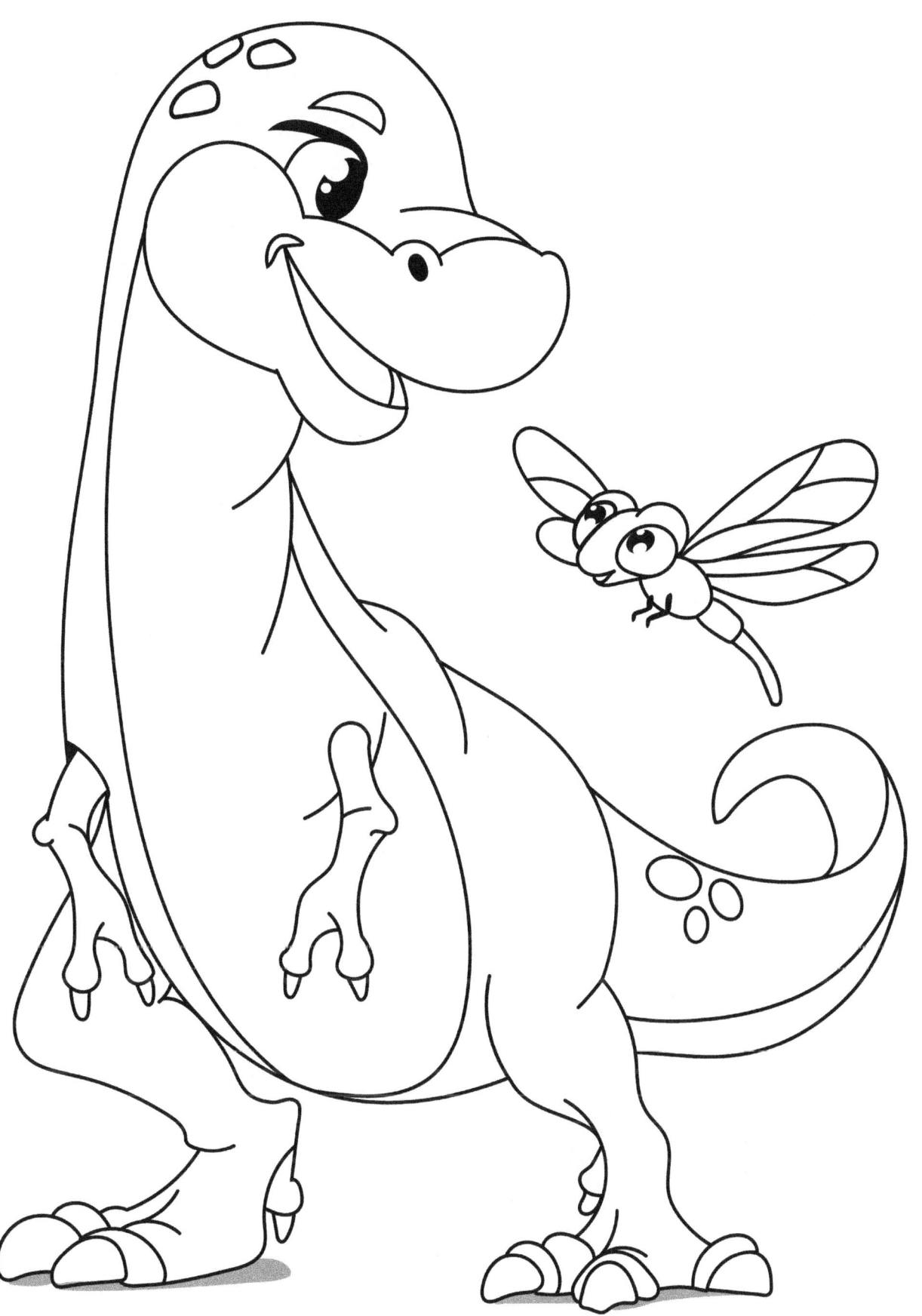

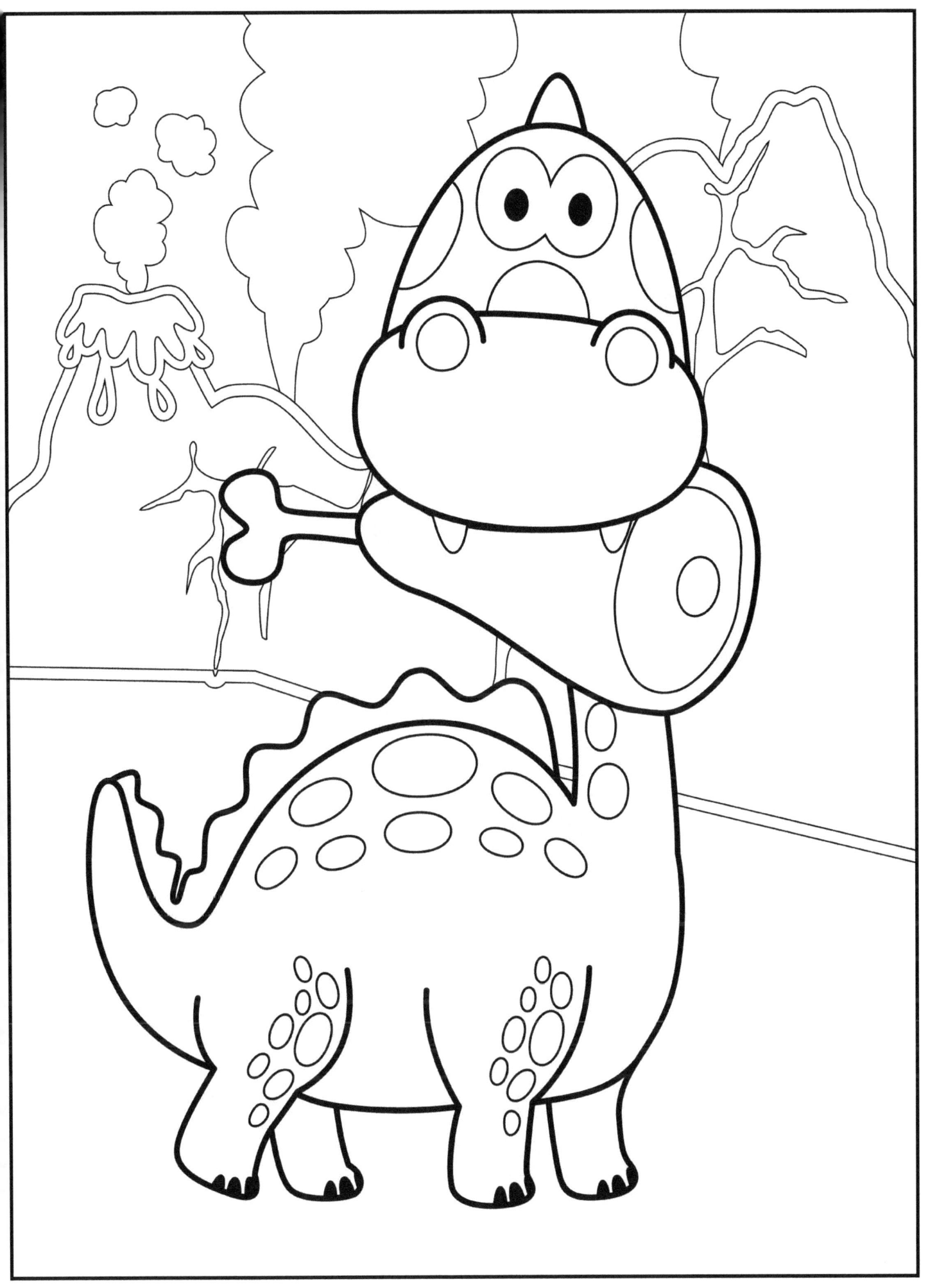

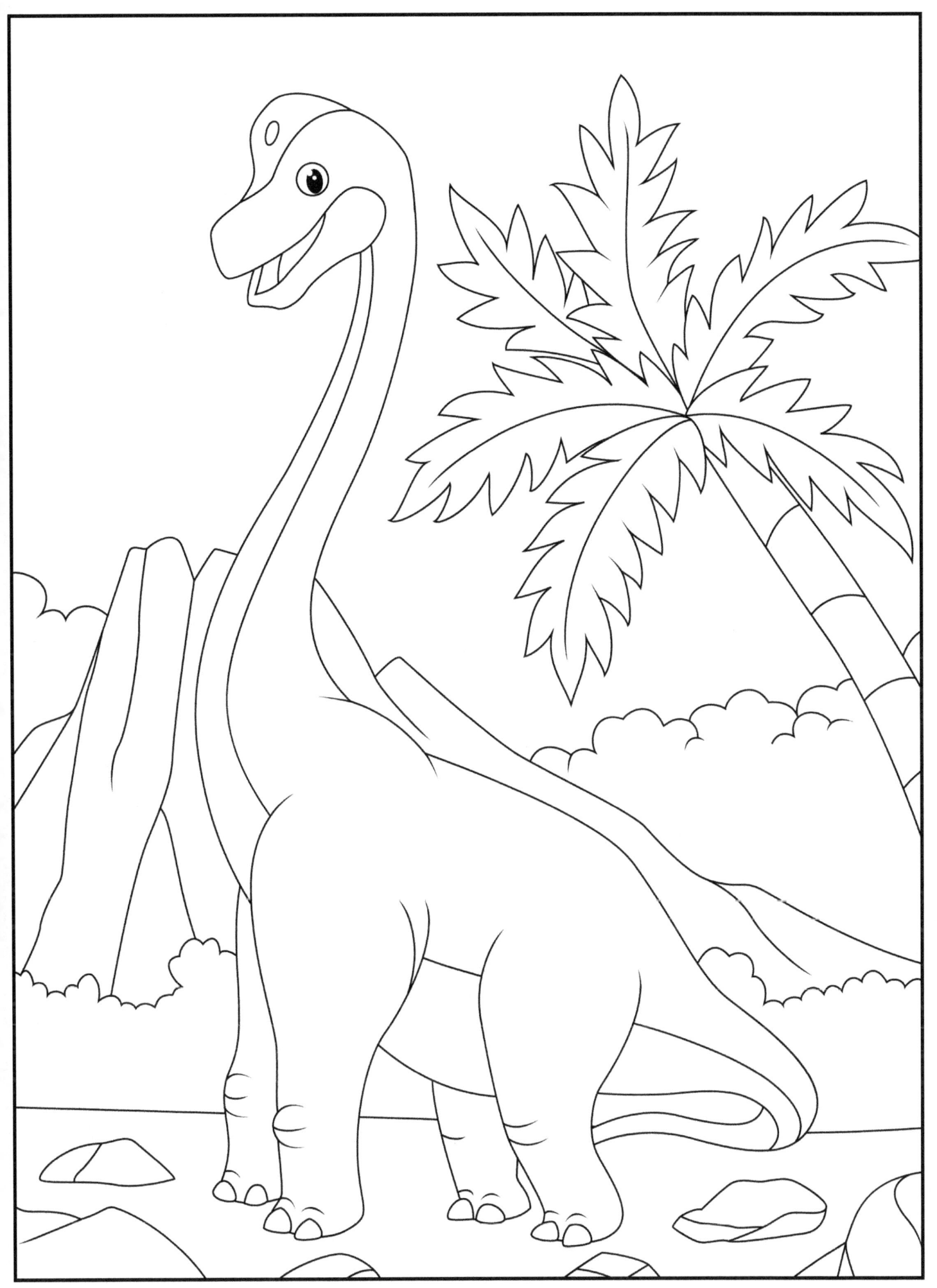

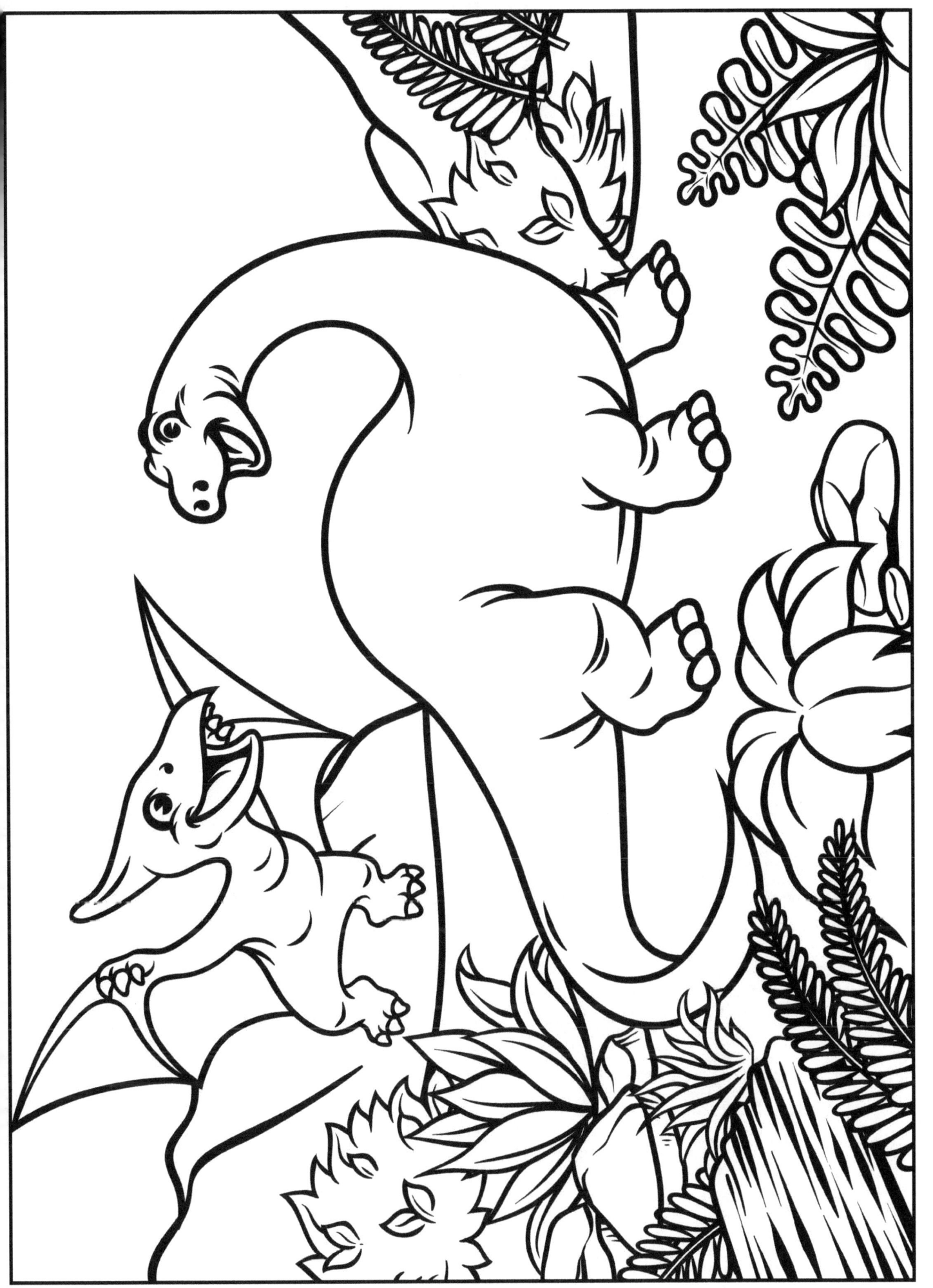

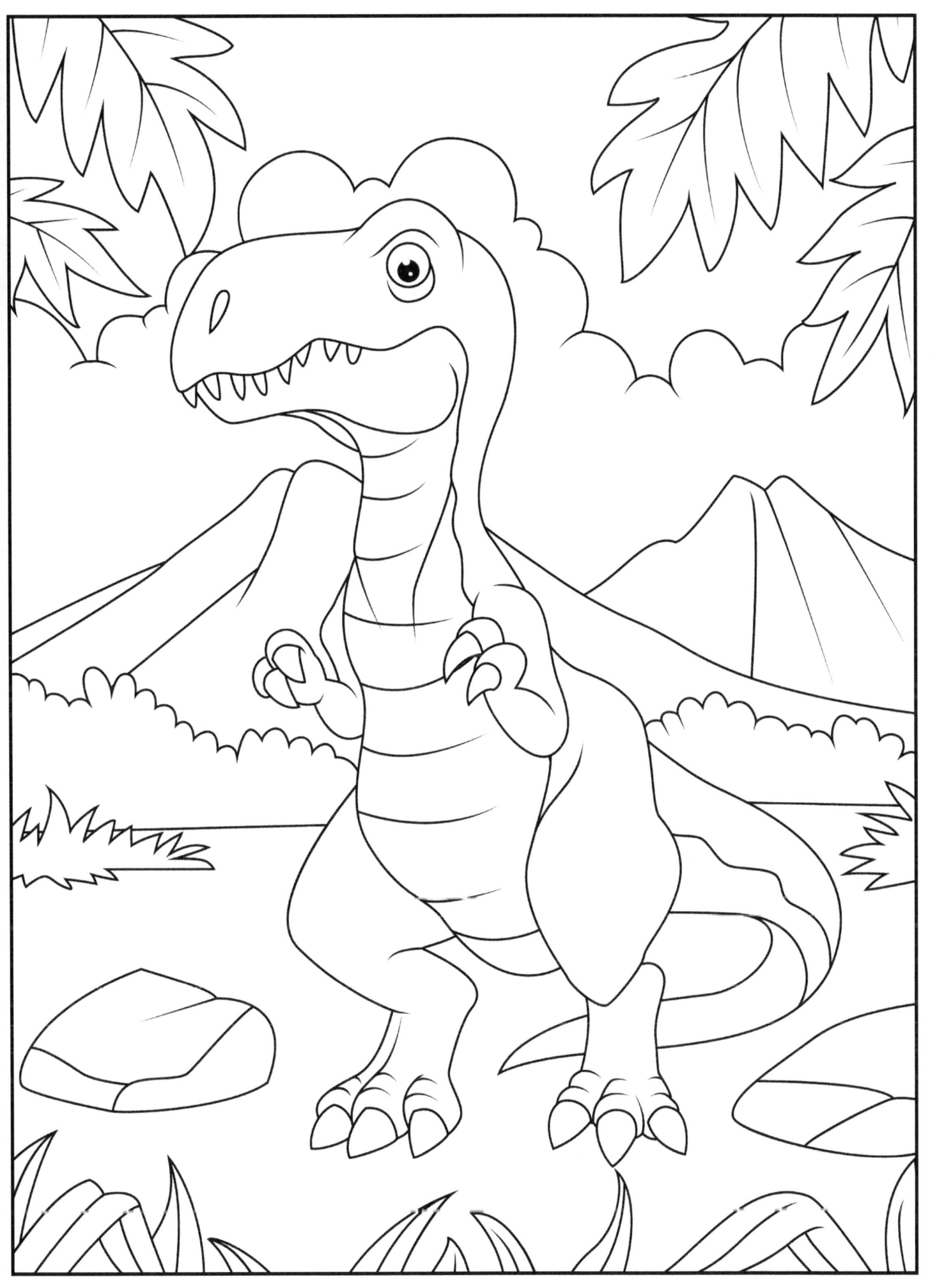

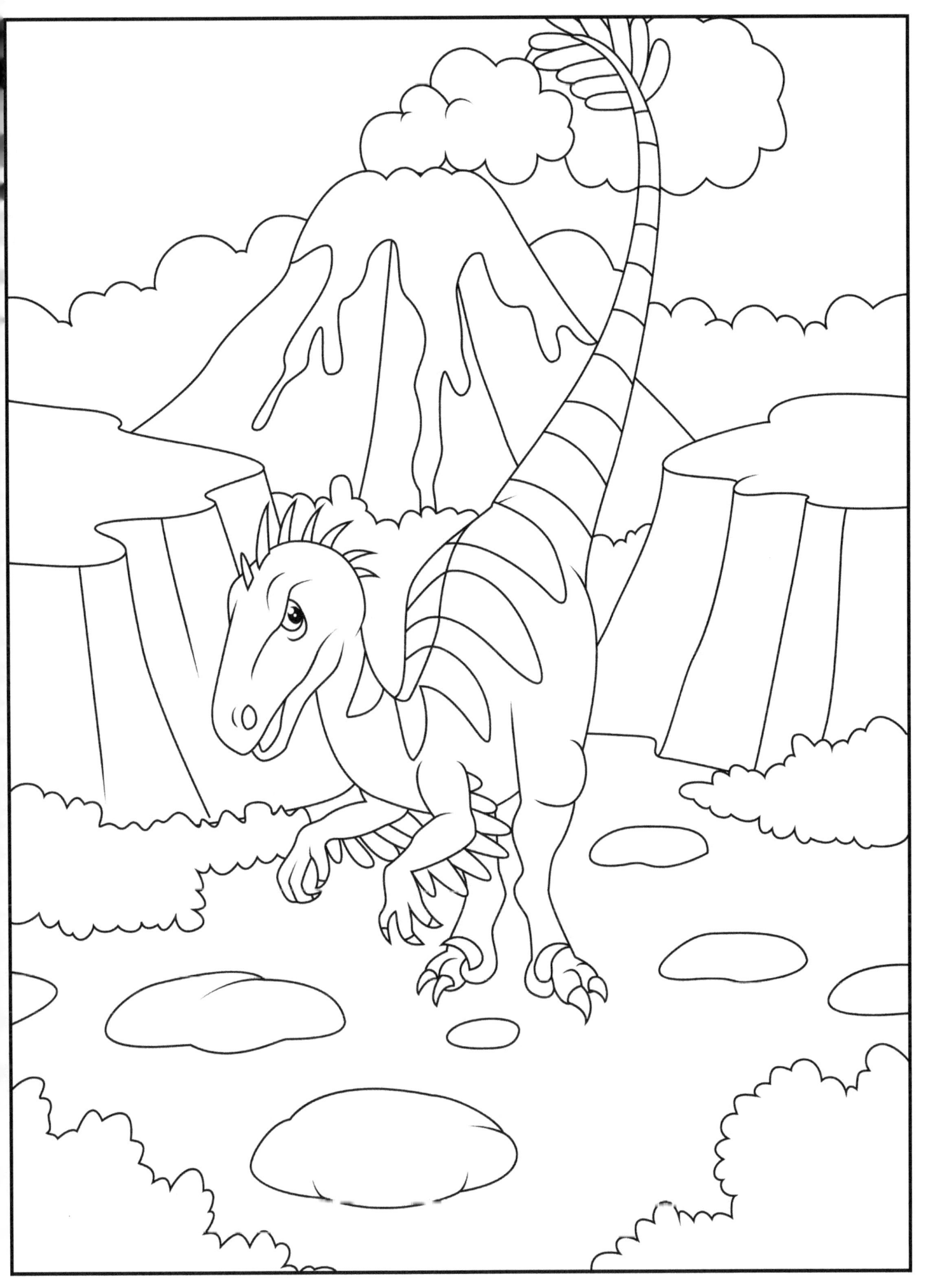

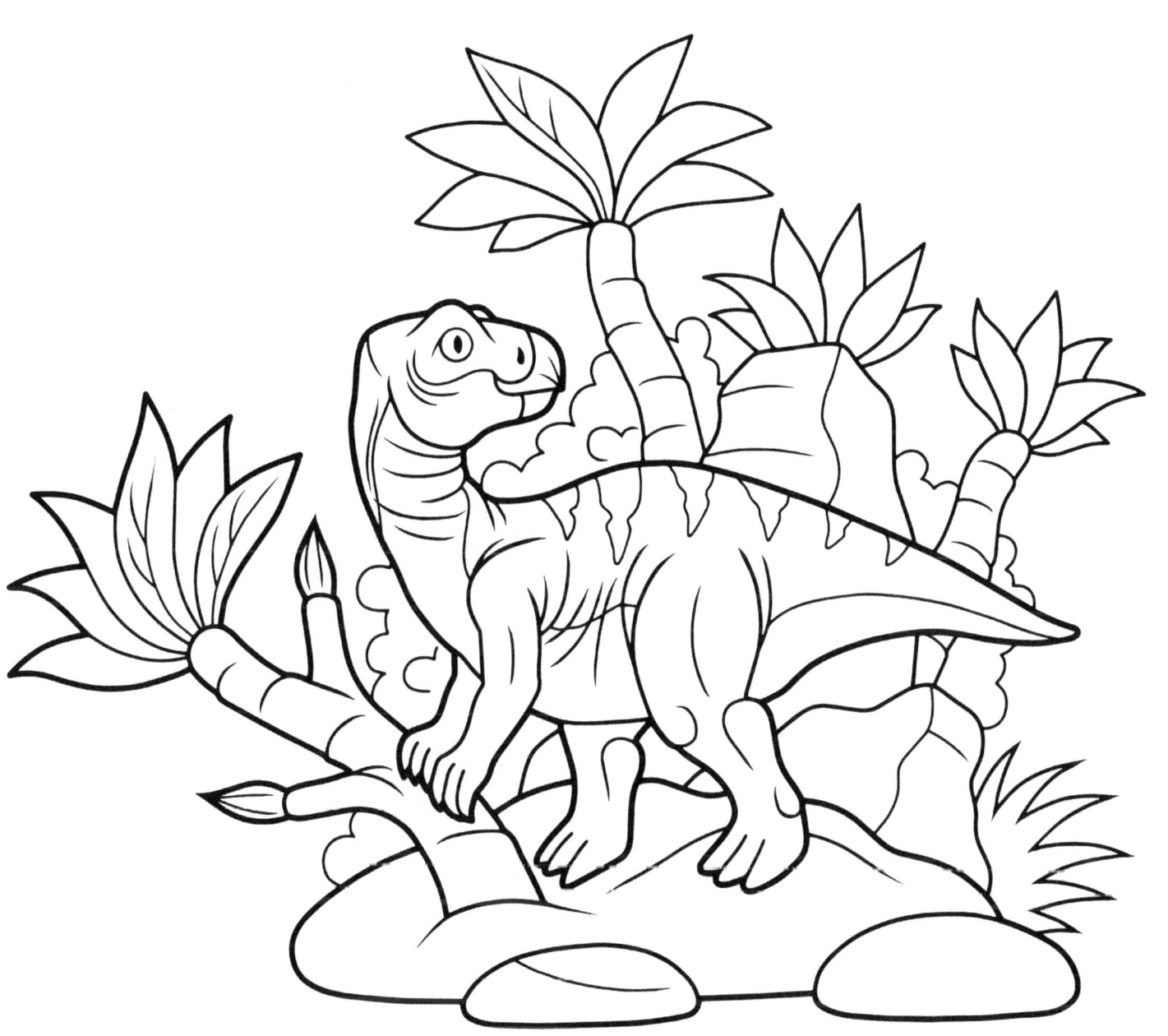

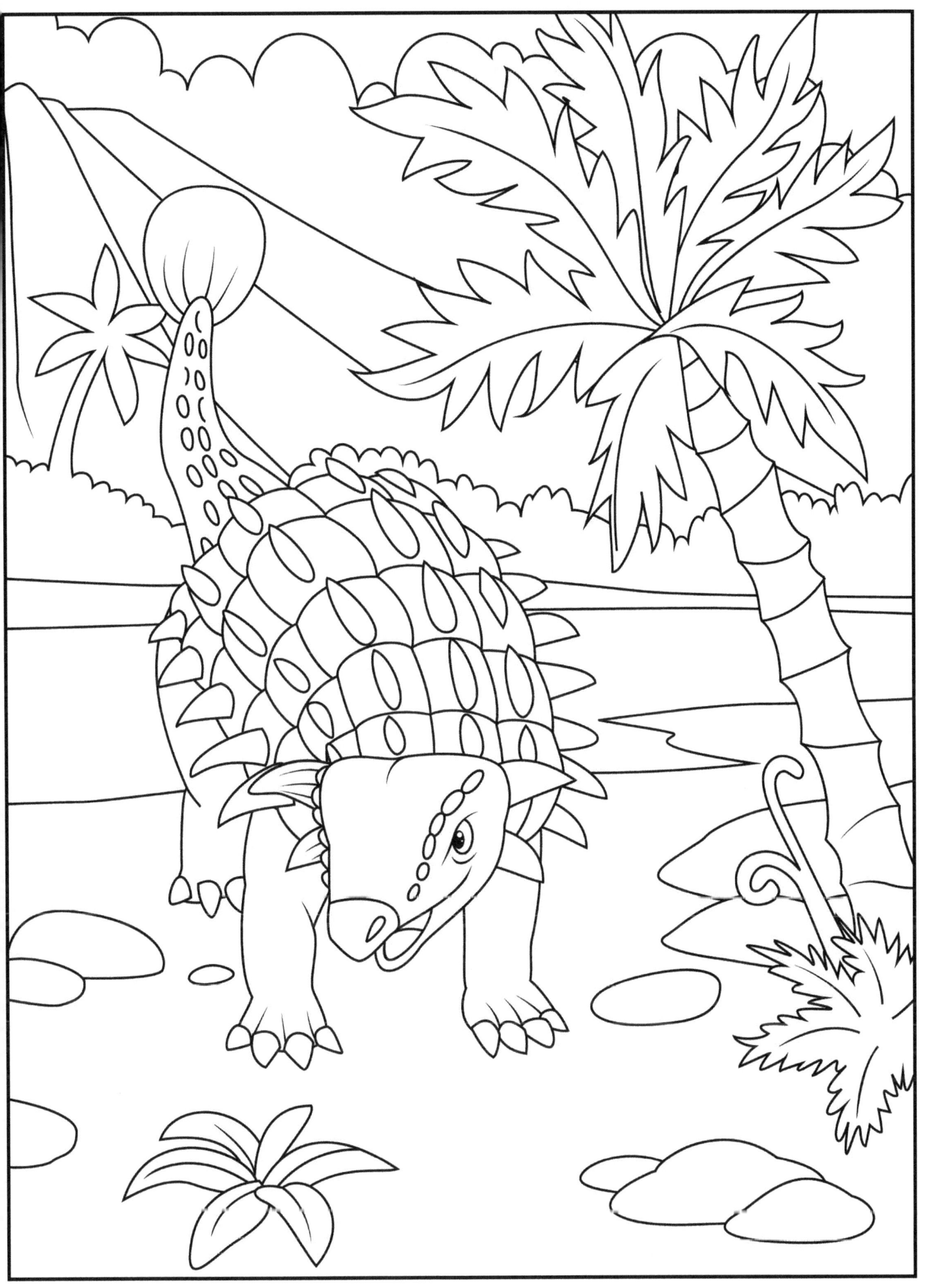

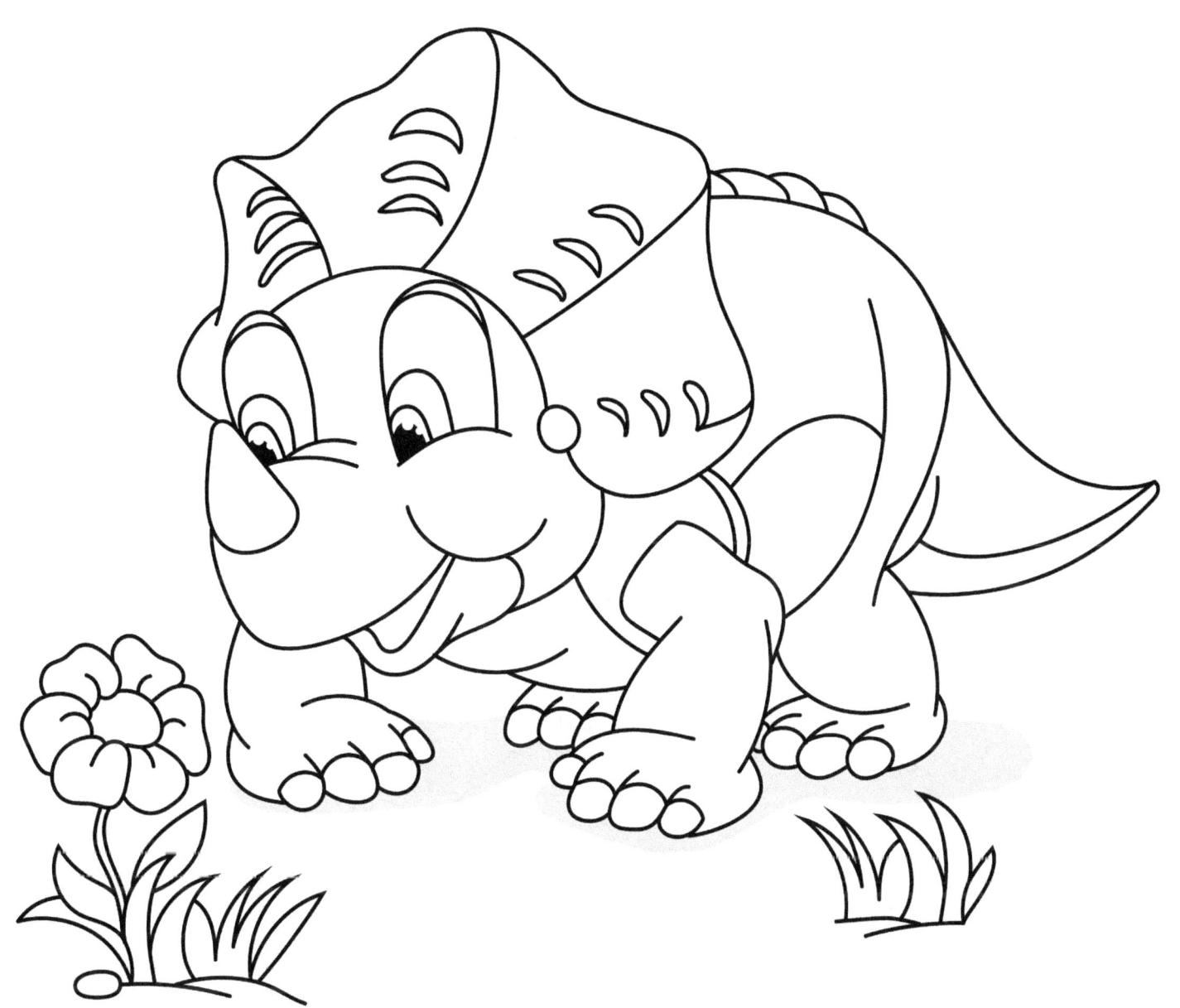

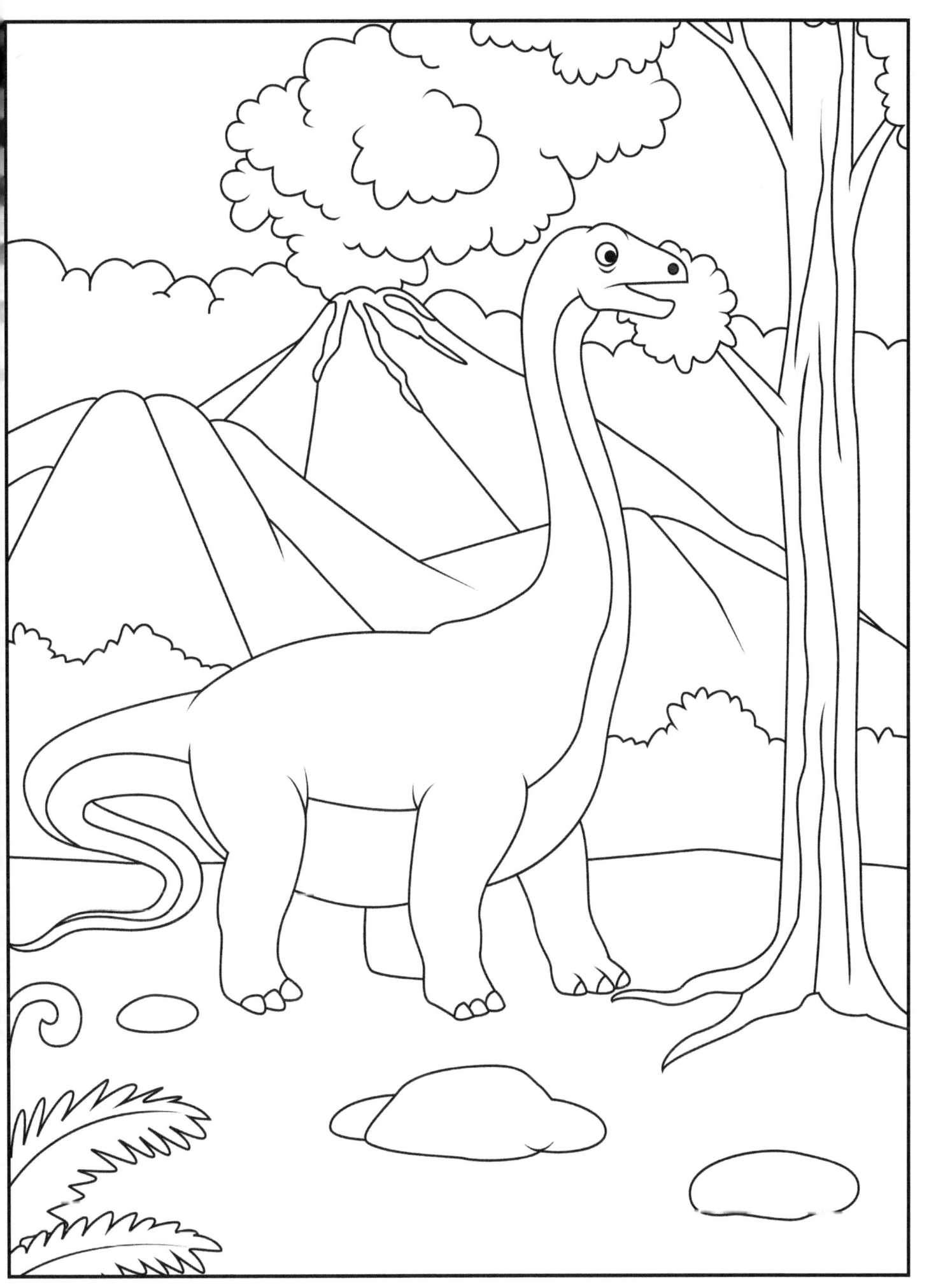

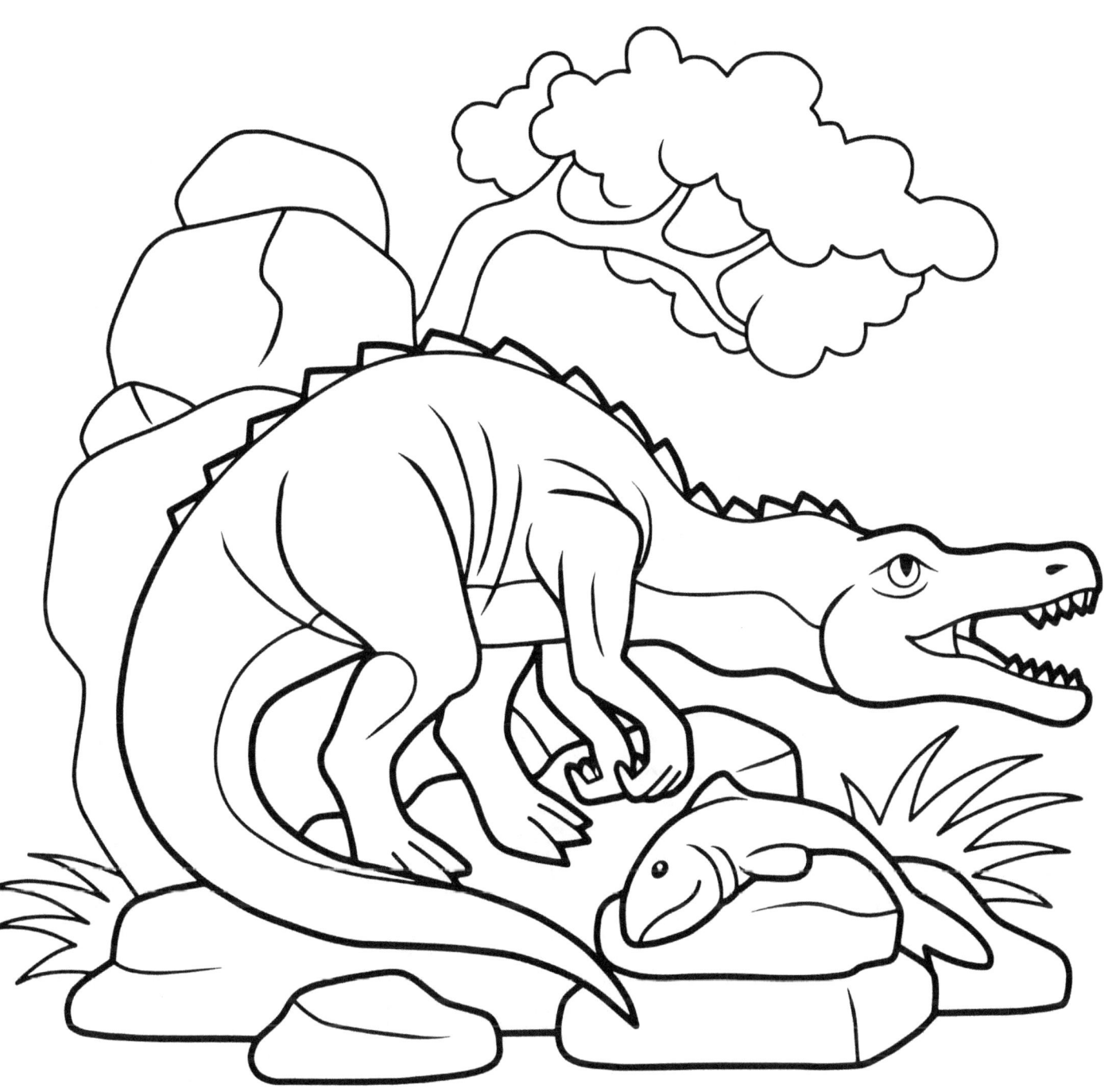

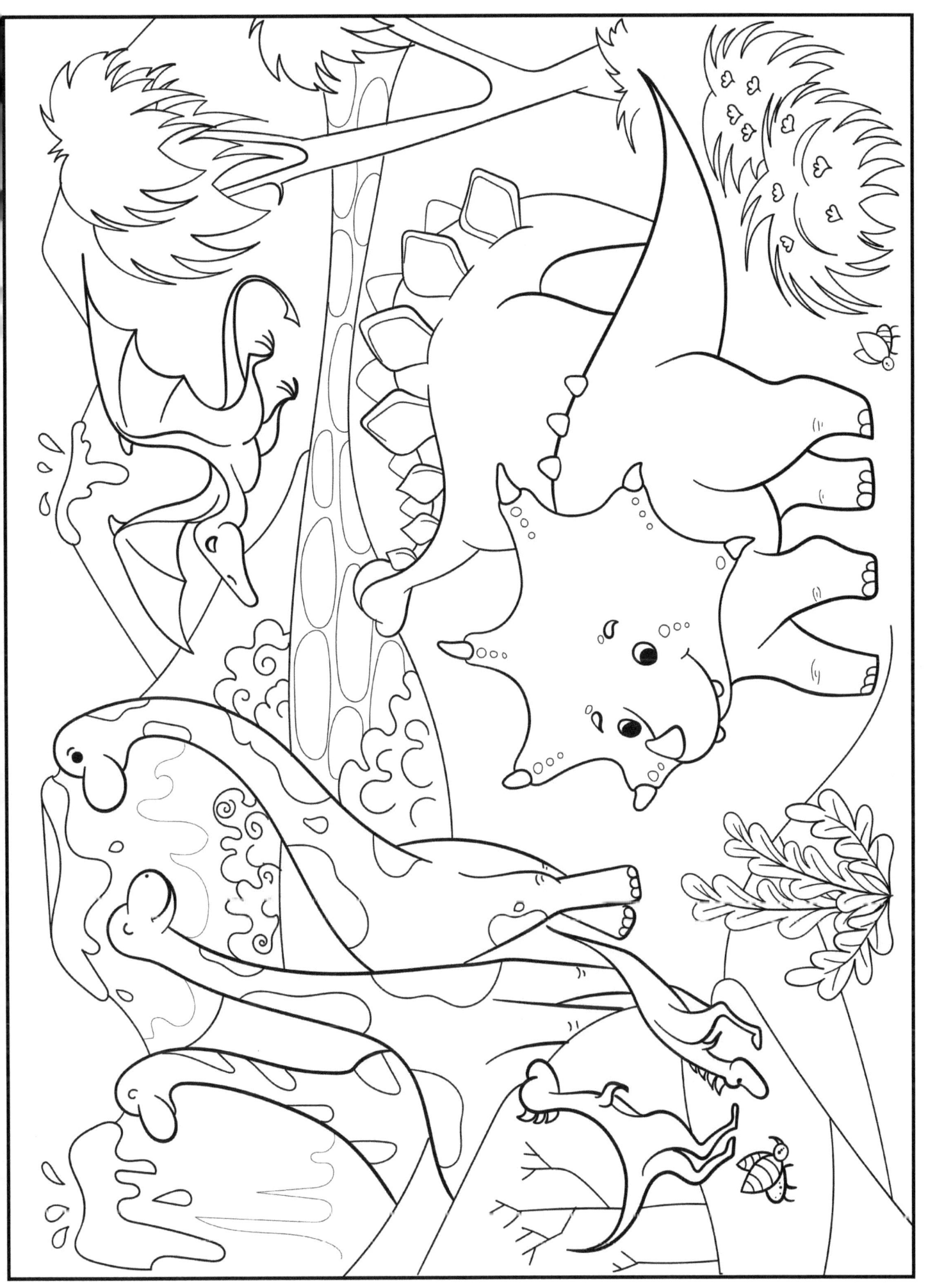

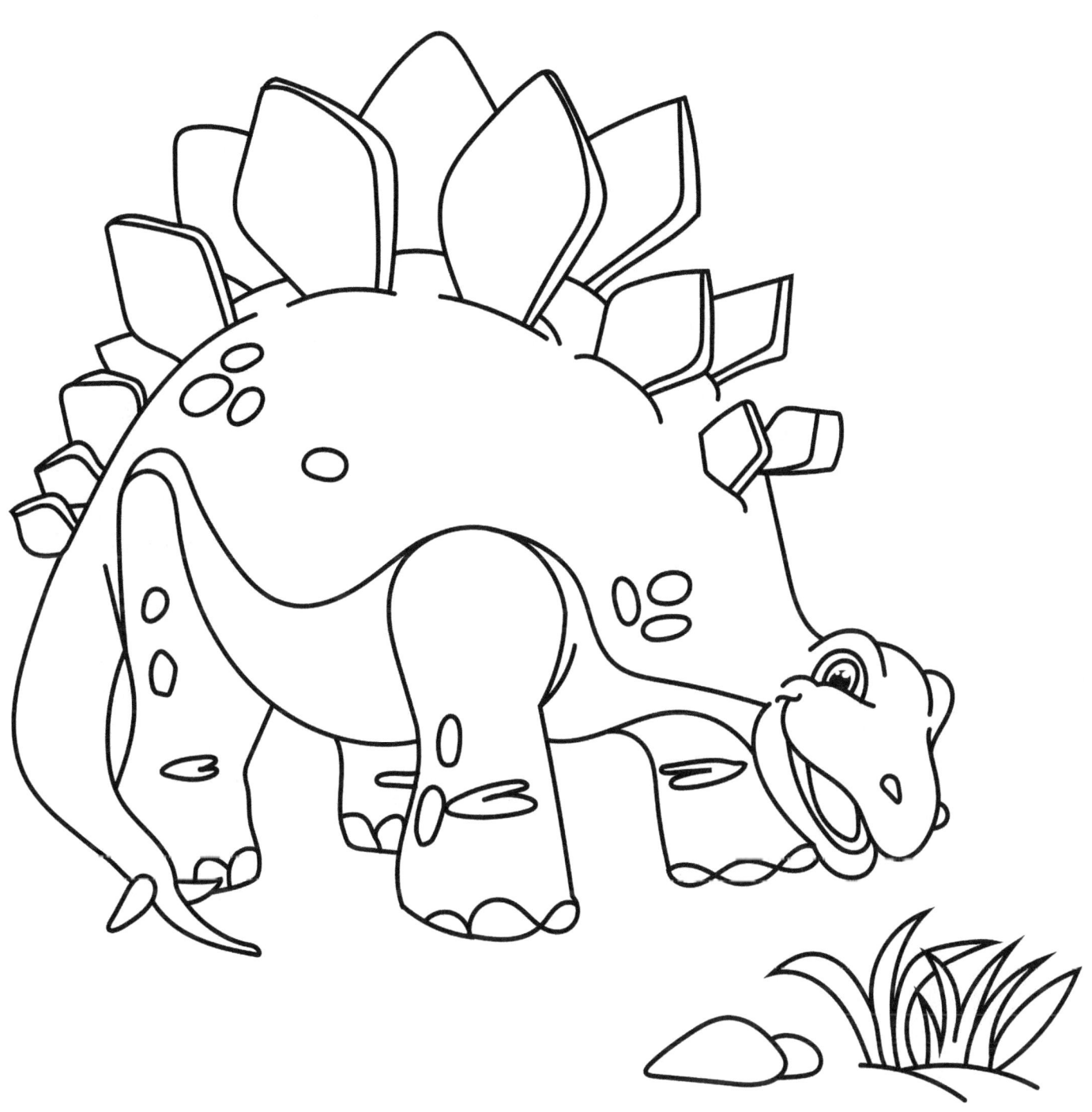

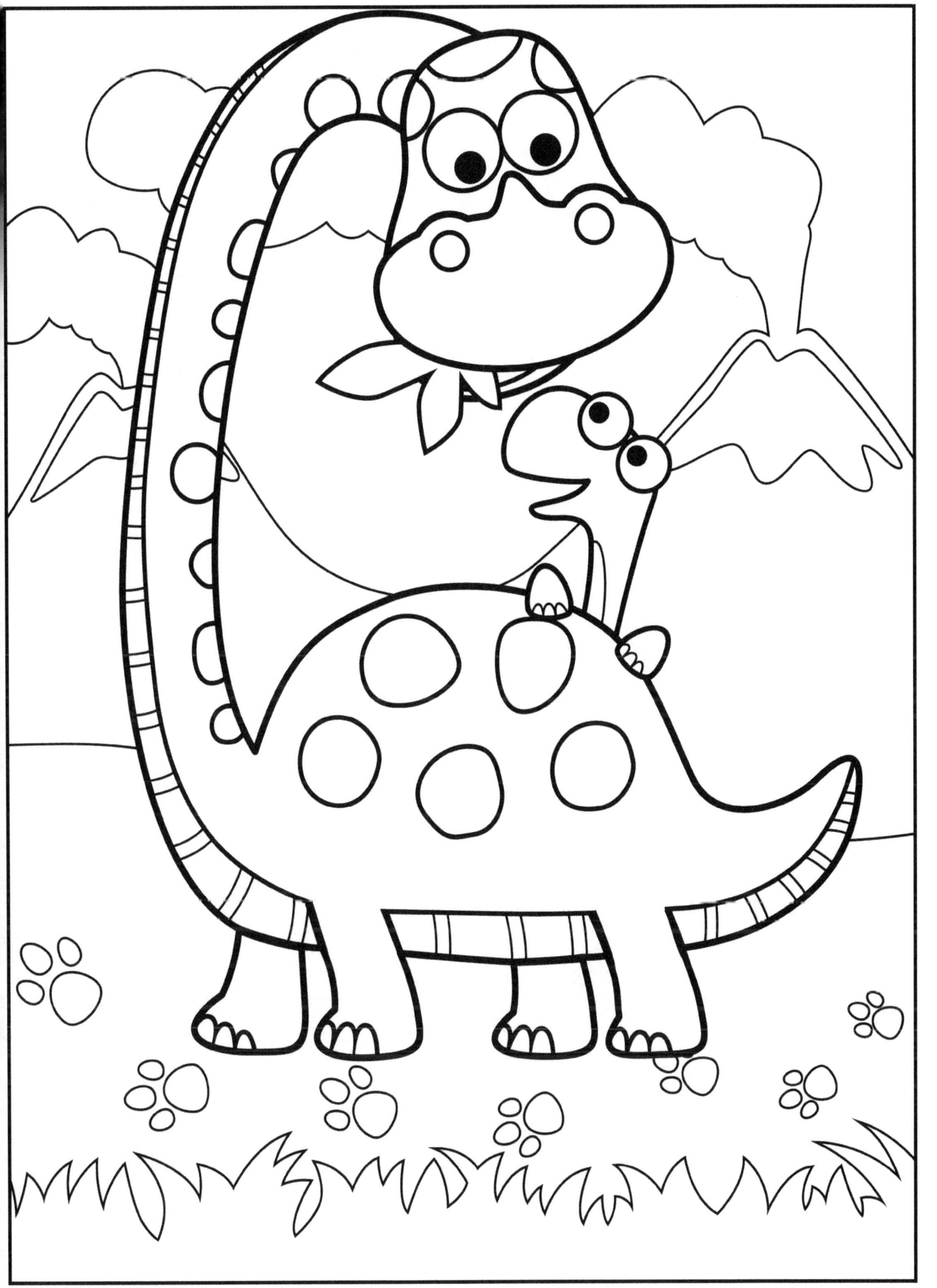

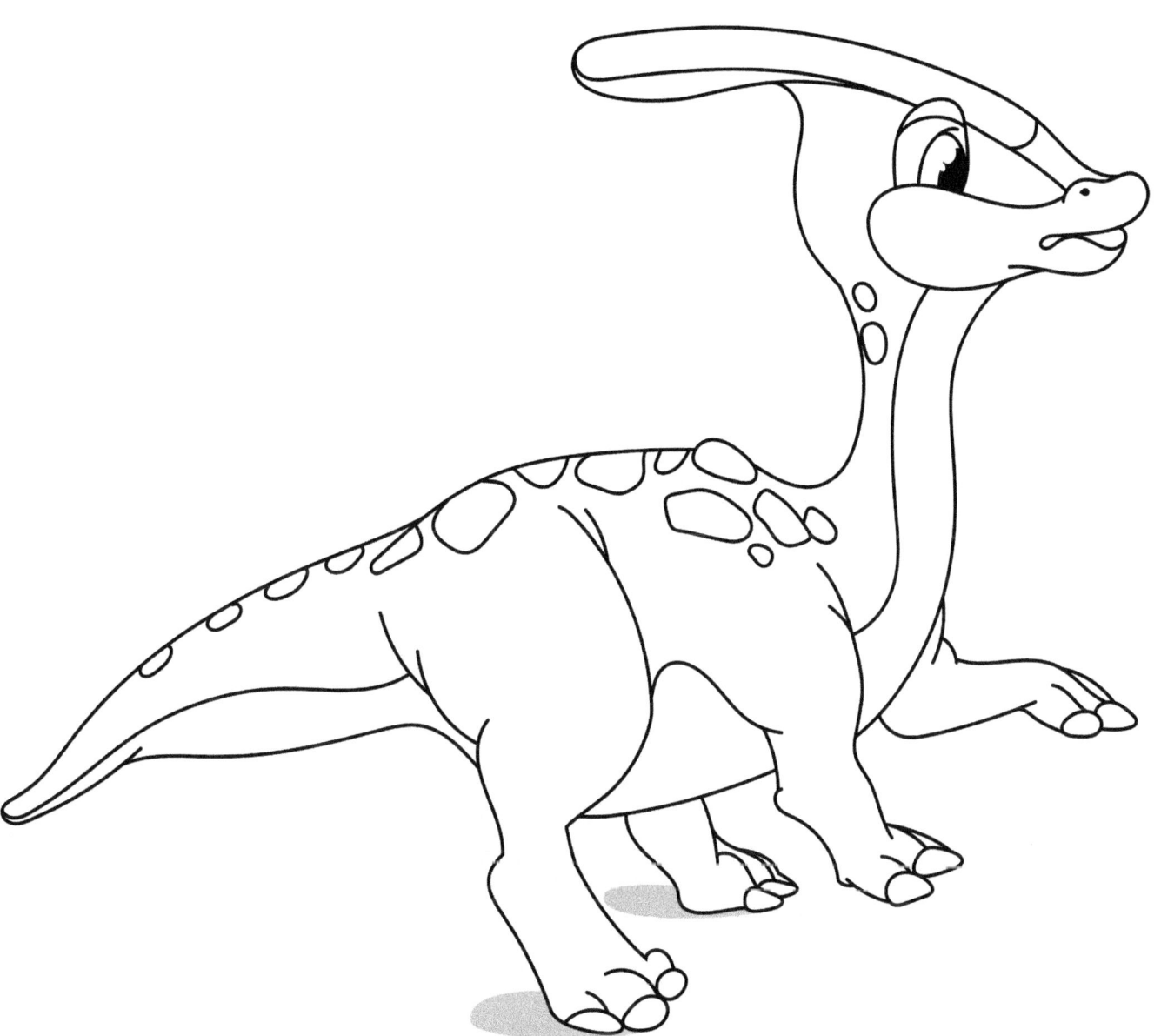

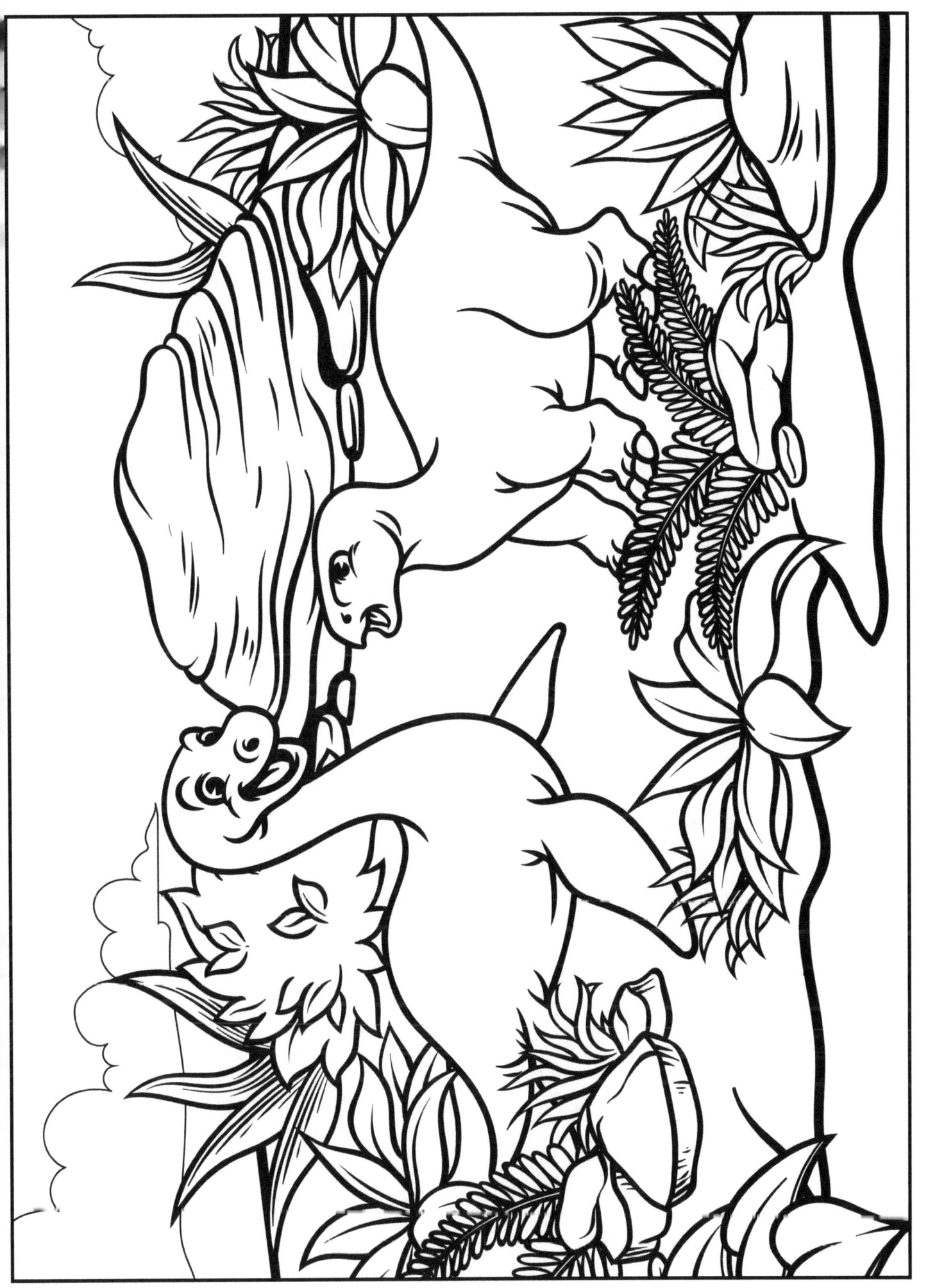

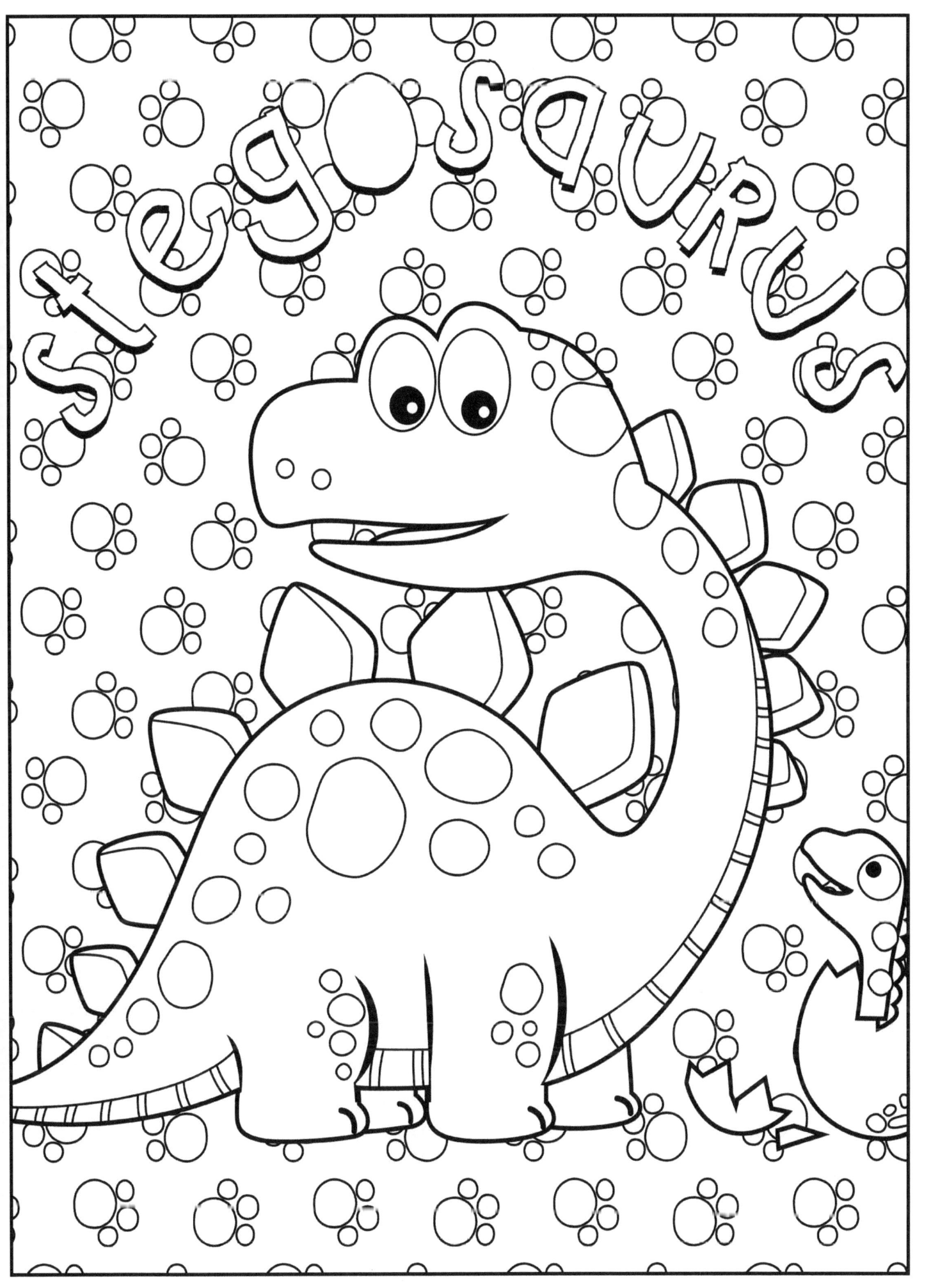

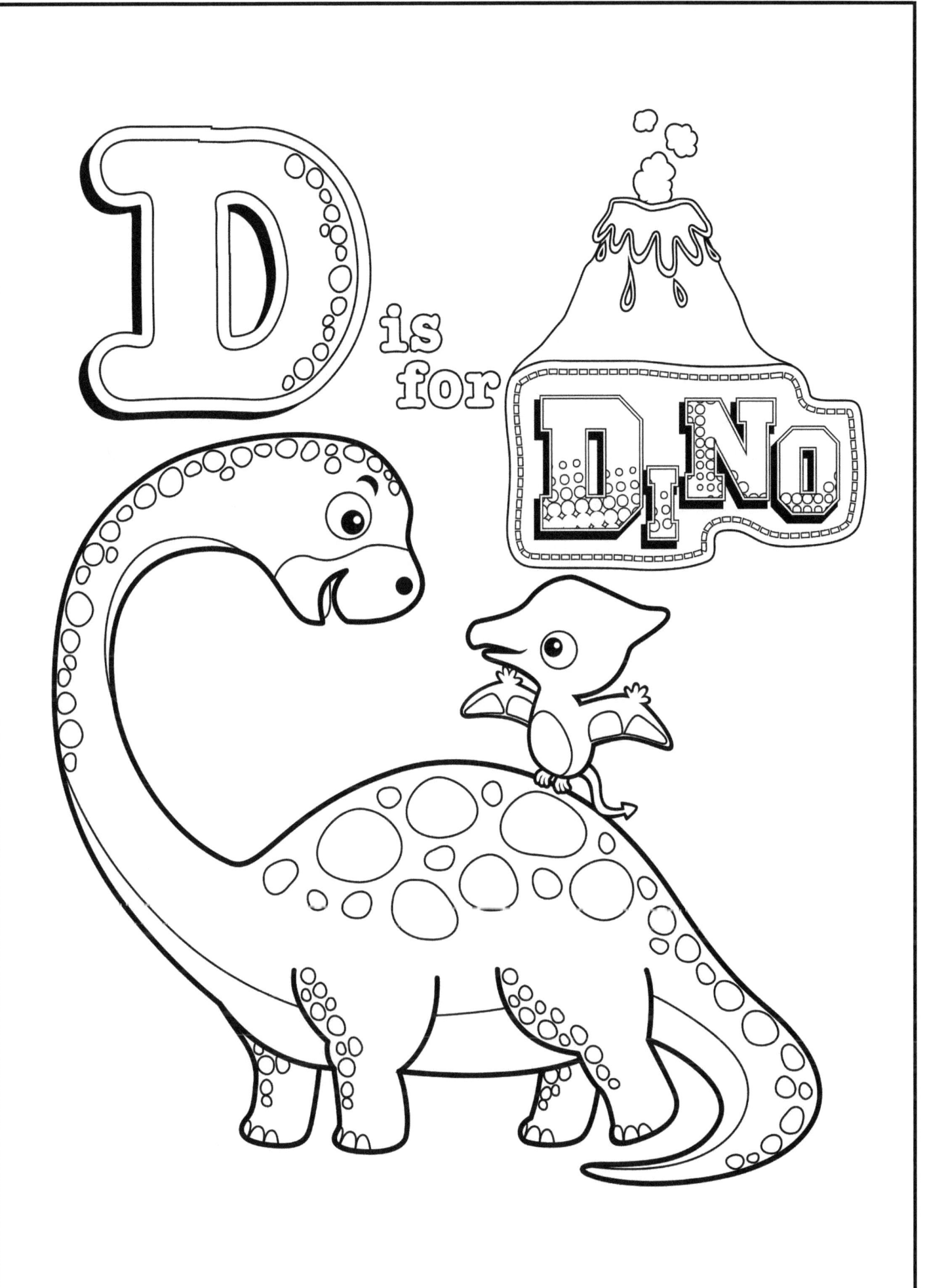

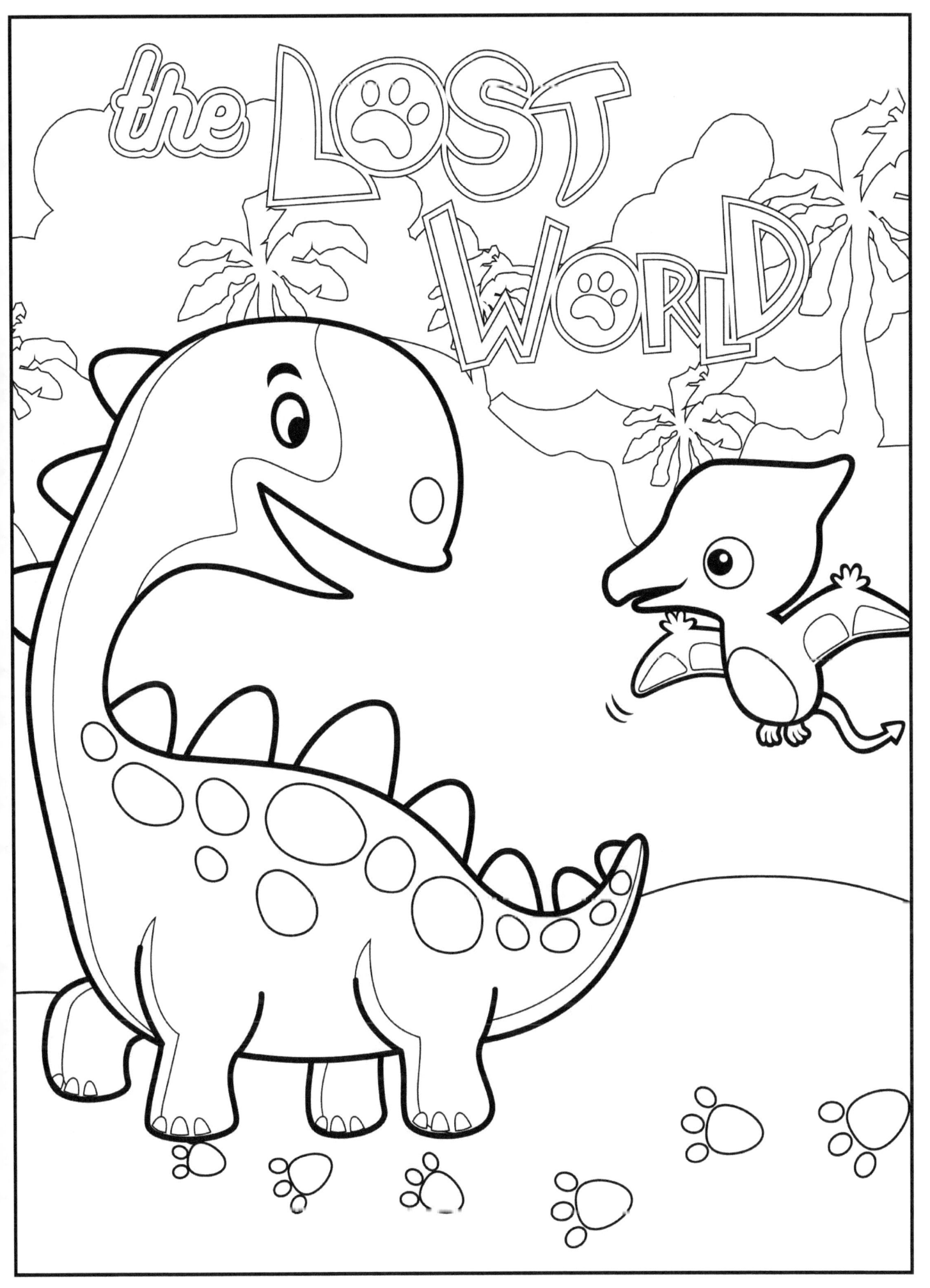

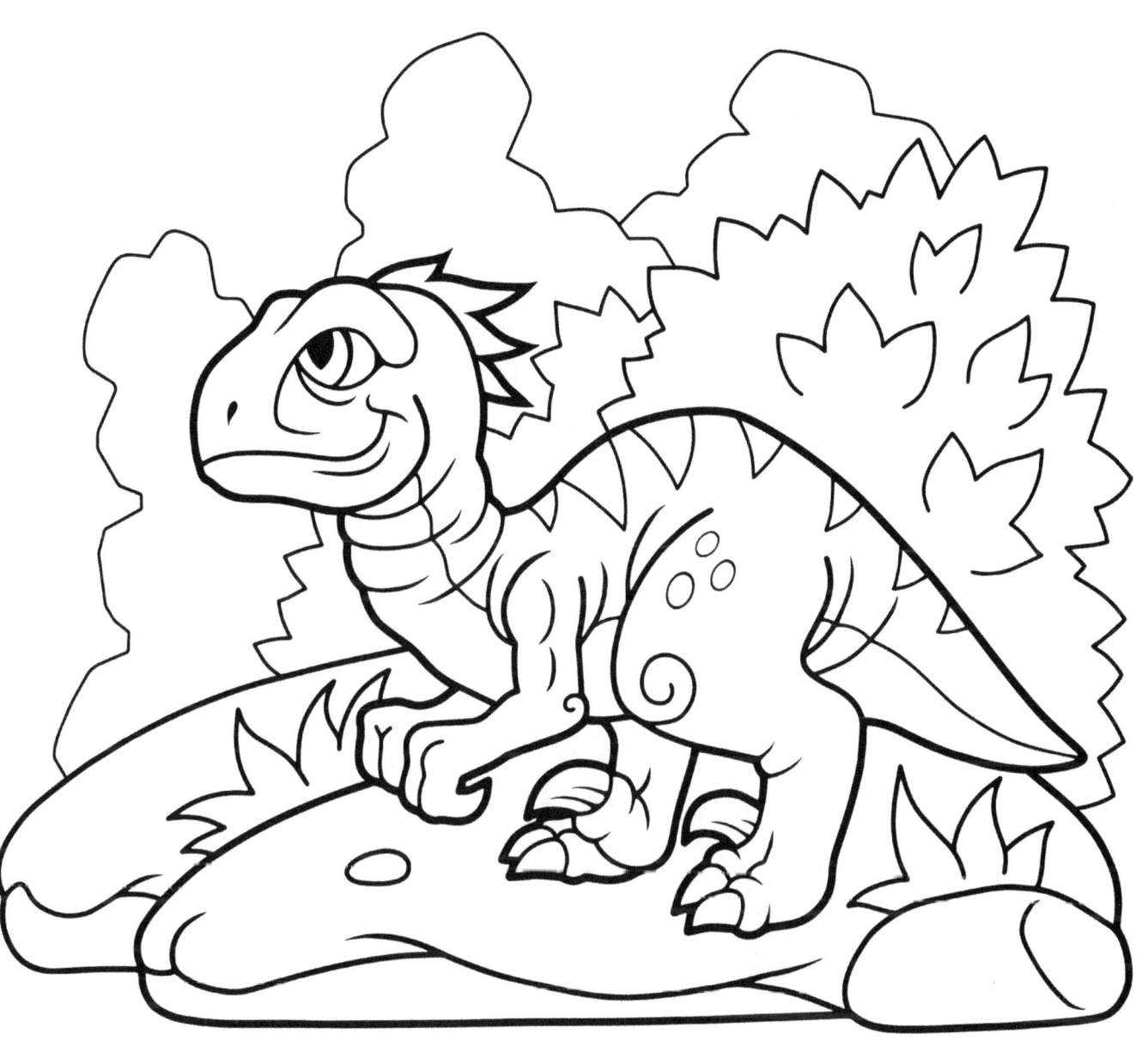

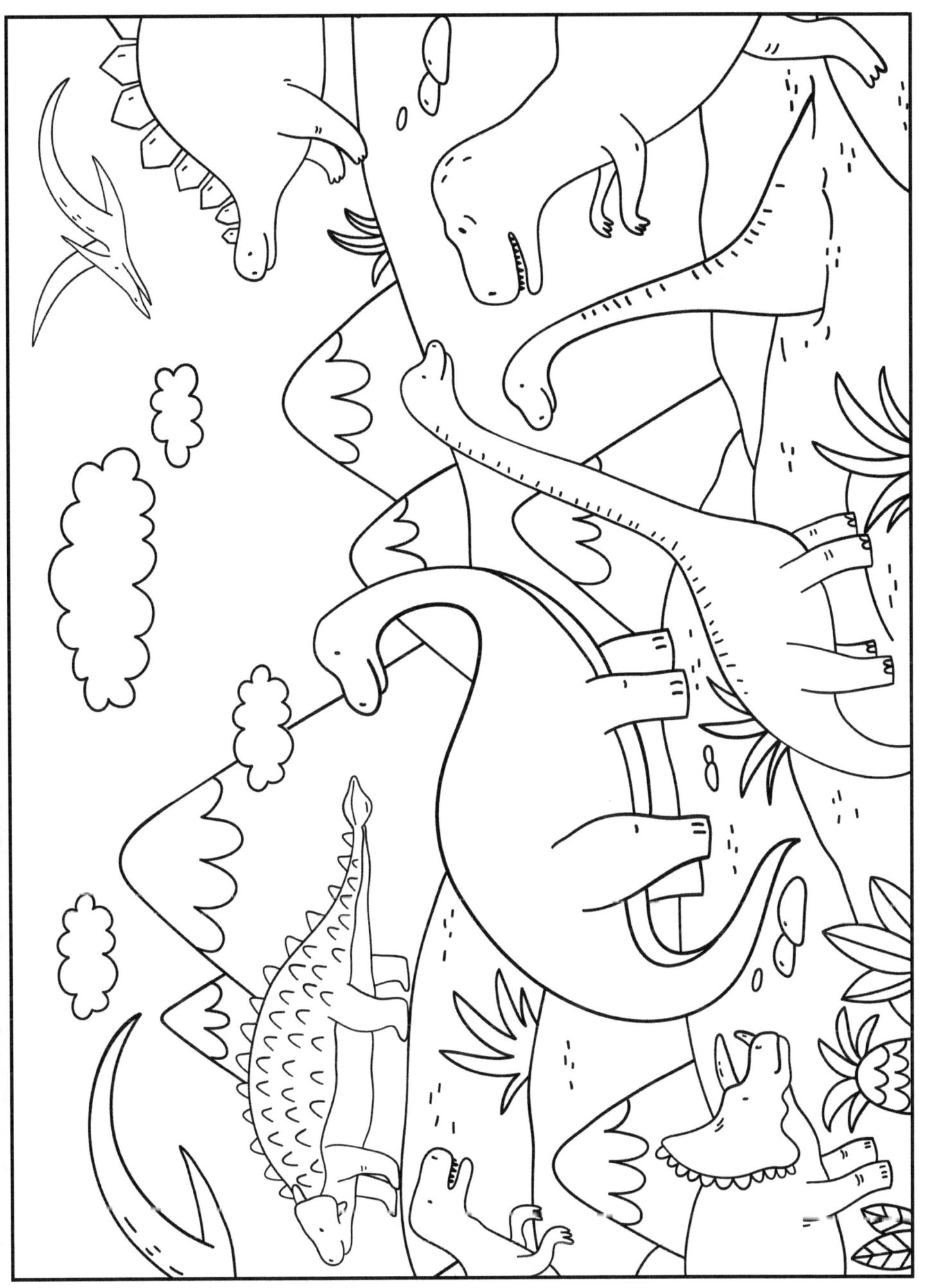

Bonus

Turn the page for bonus pages from some of our most popular coloring and activity books.

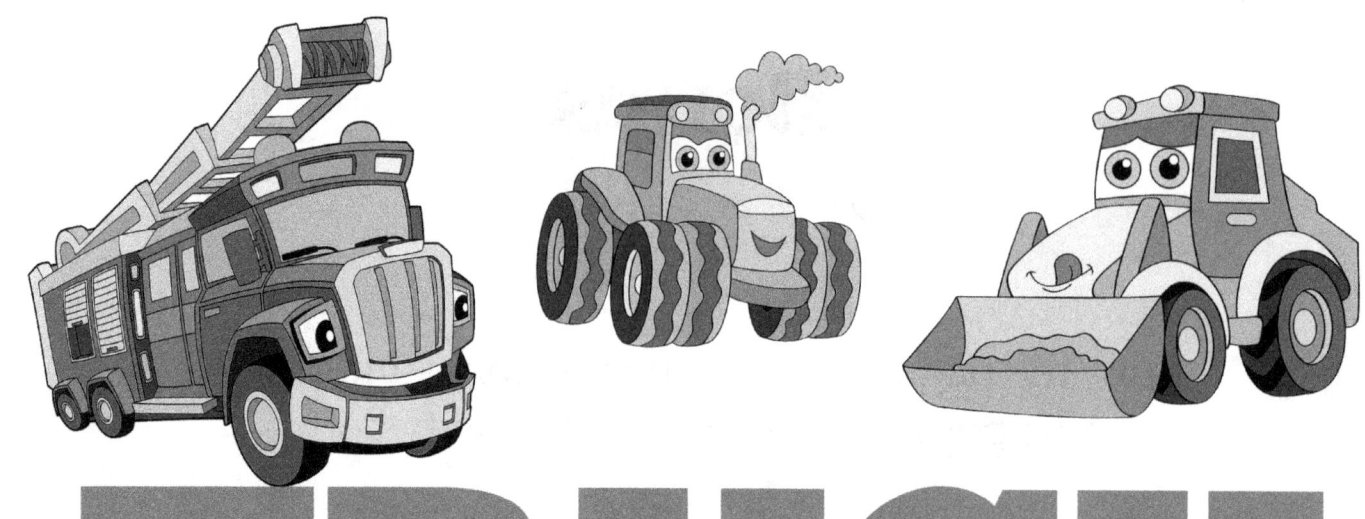

TRUCK
COLORING BOOK

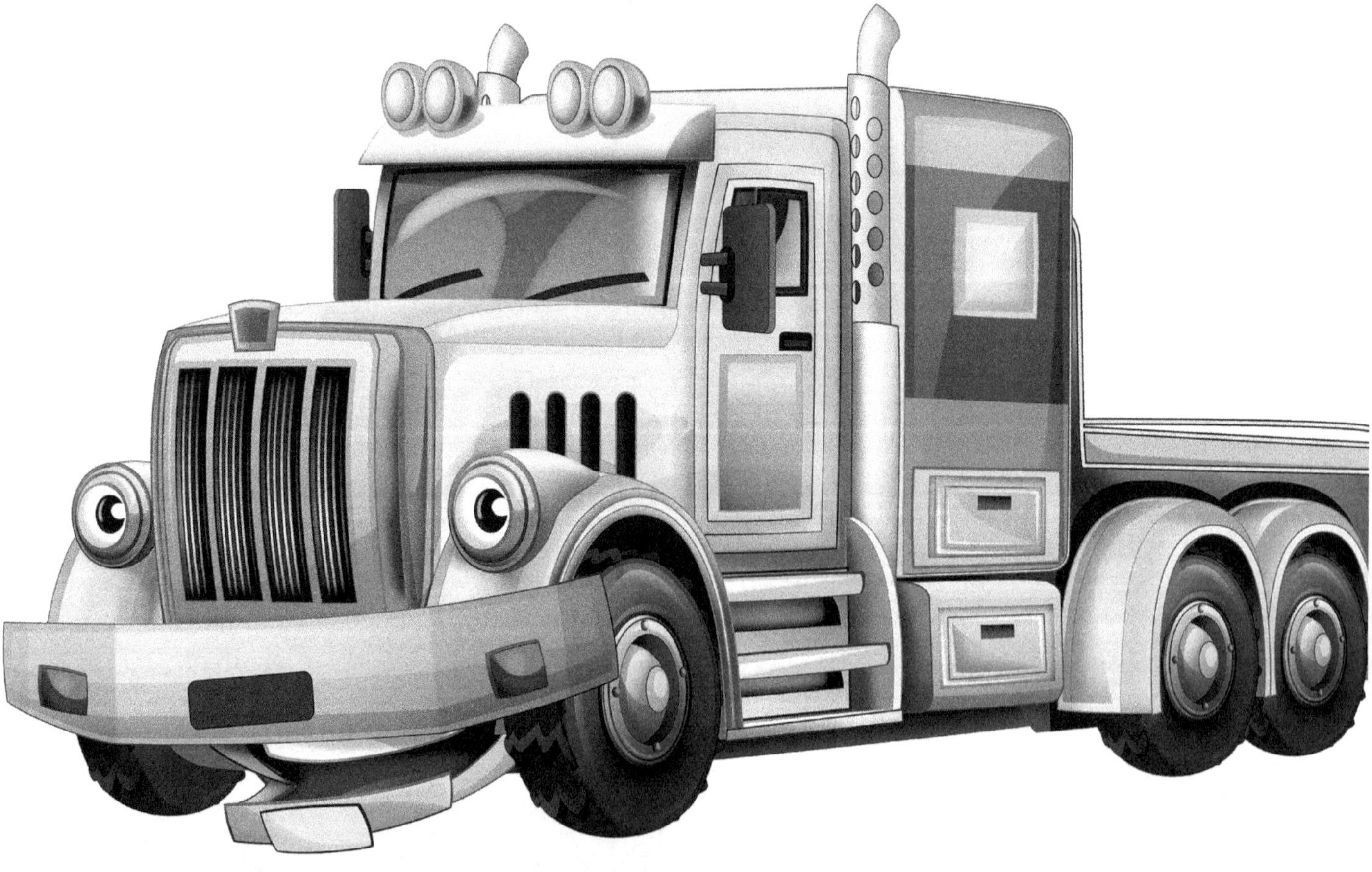

COLORING BOOKS FOR KIDS

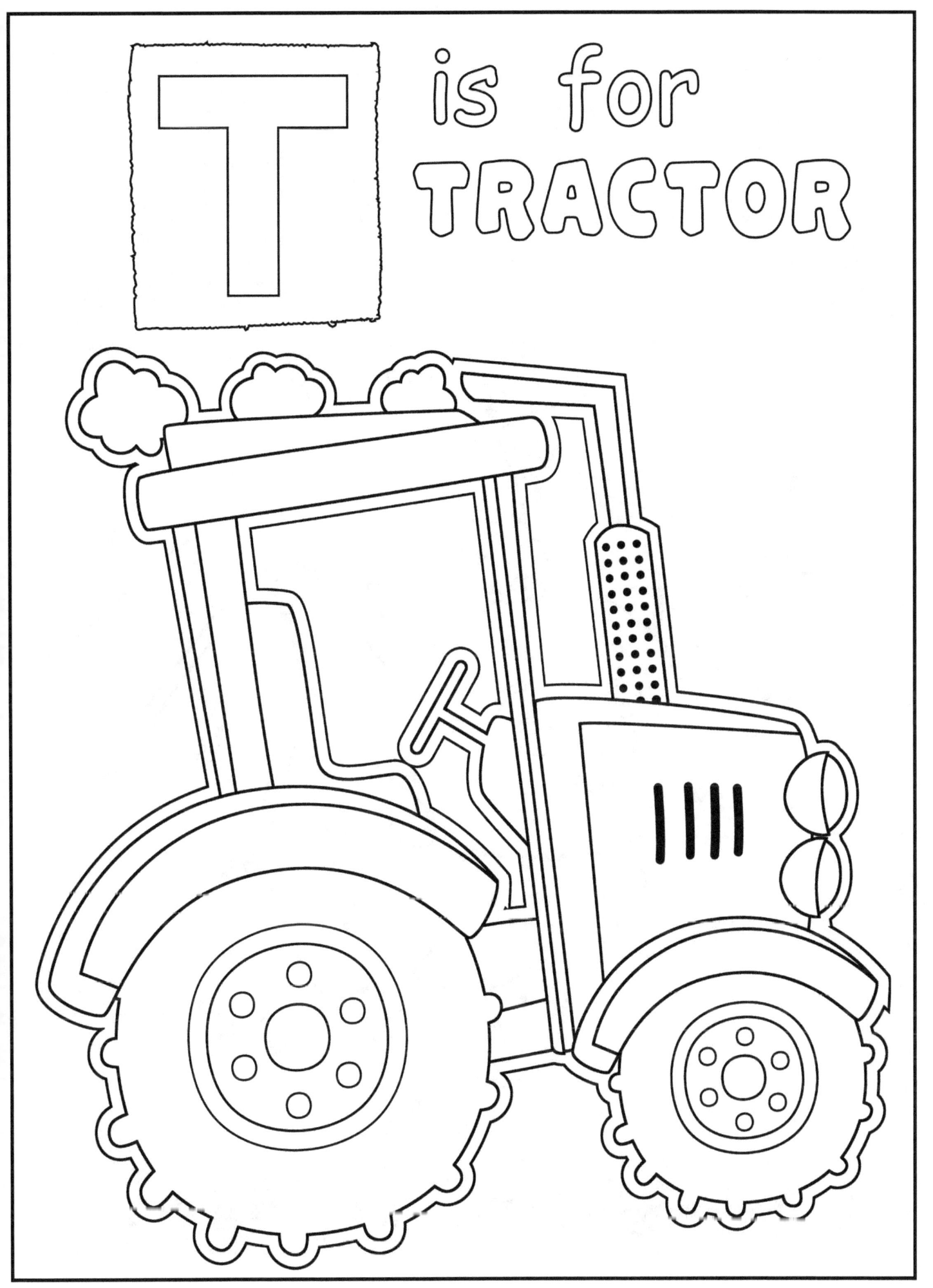

Connect the Dots
Book for Kids

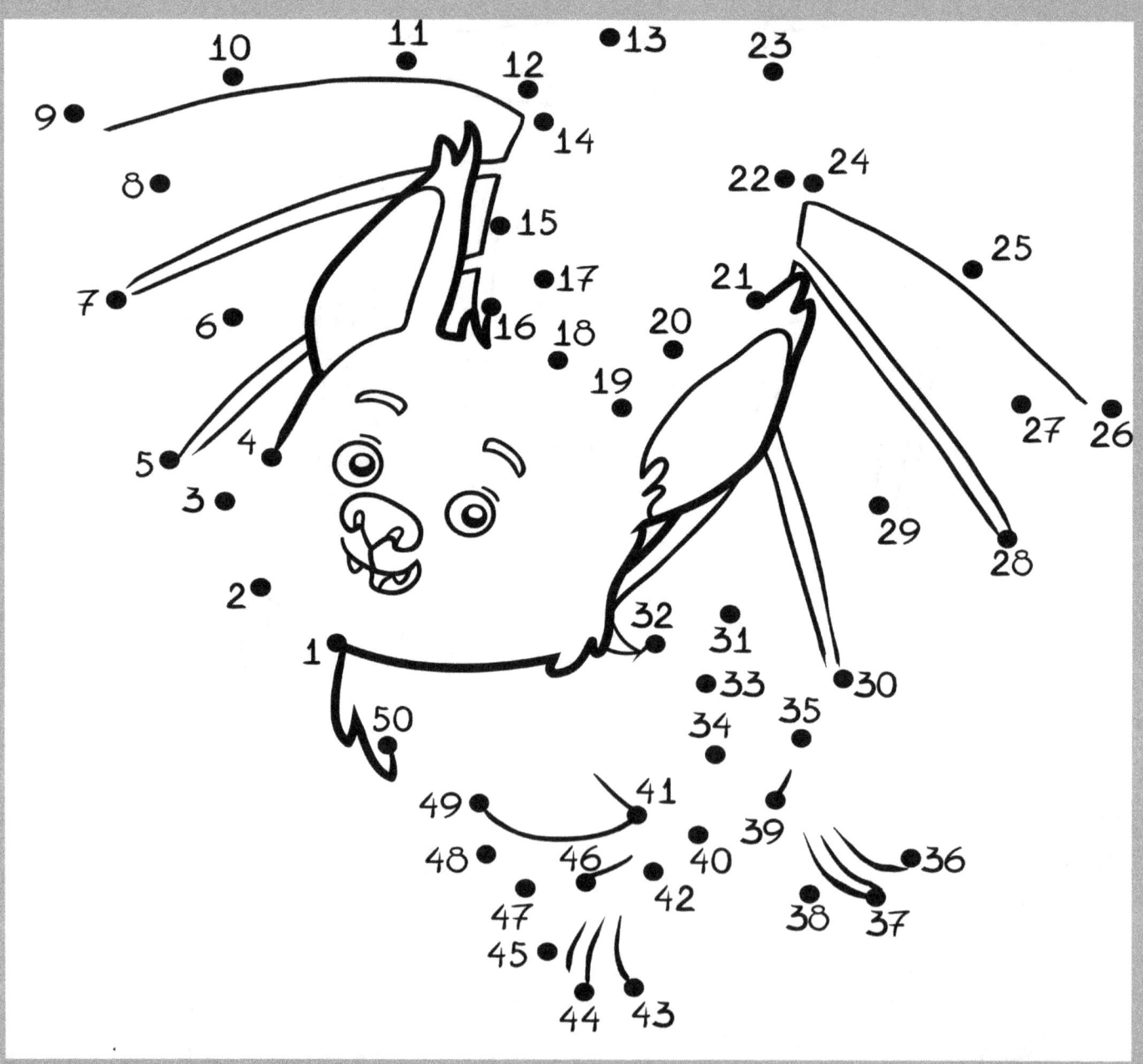

Challenging and Fun Dot to Dot Puzzles

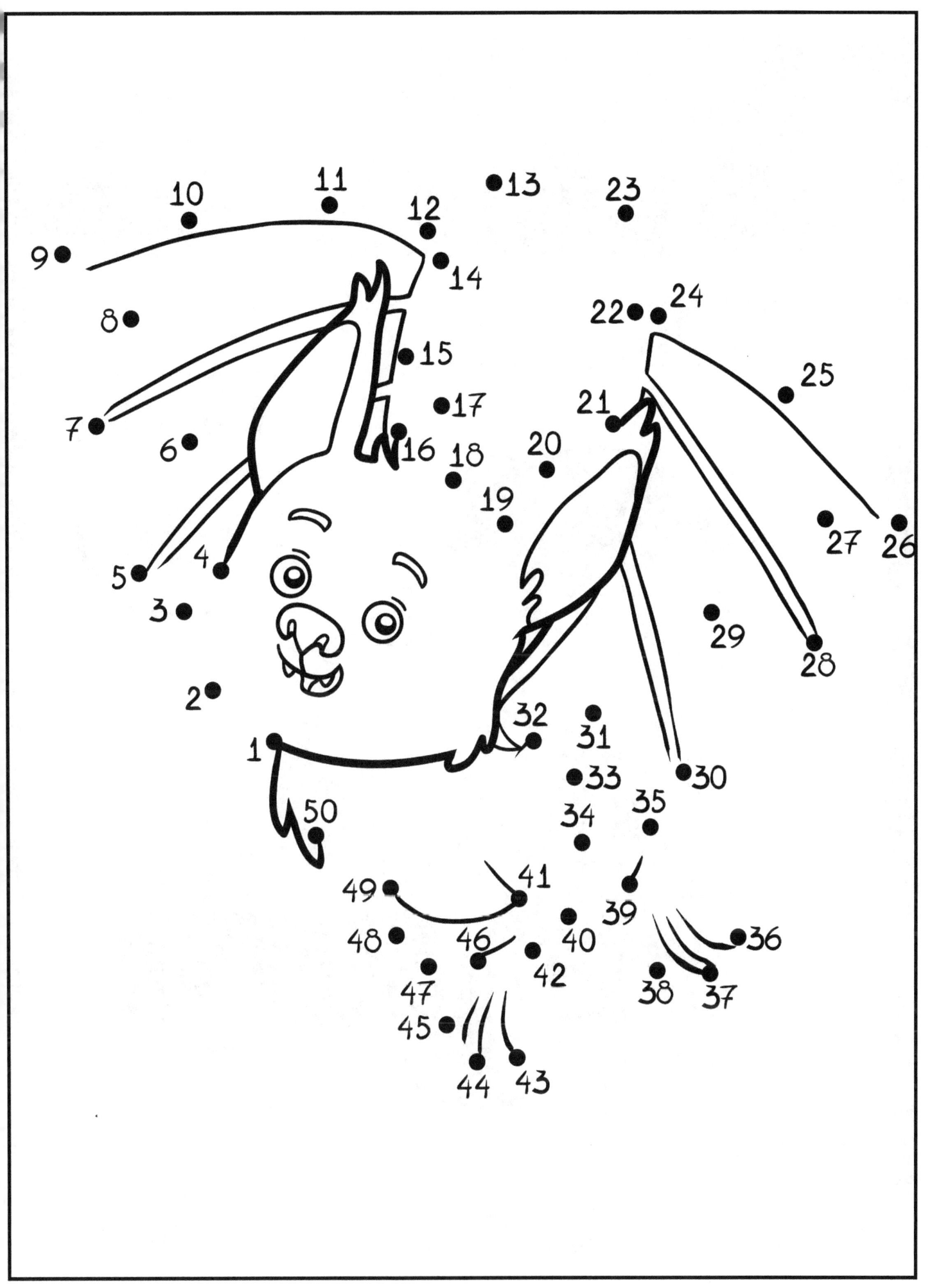

MILITARY COLORING BOOK

FOR KIDS

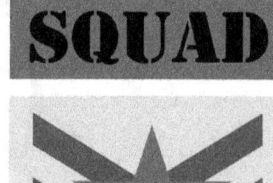

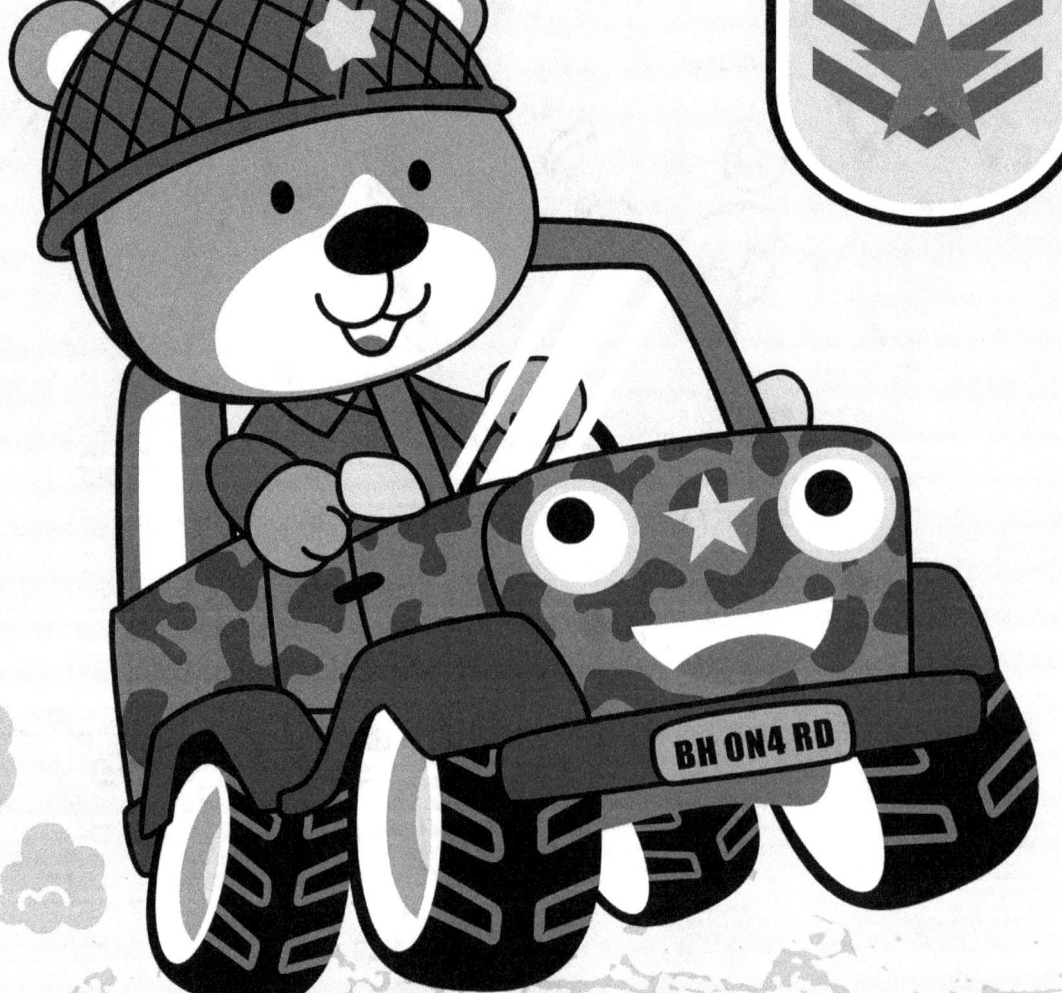

ARMY, NAVY, AIR FORCE

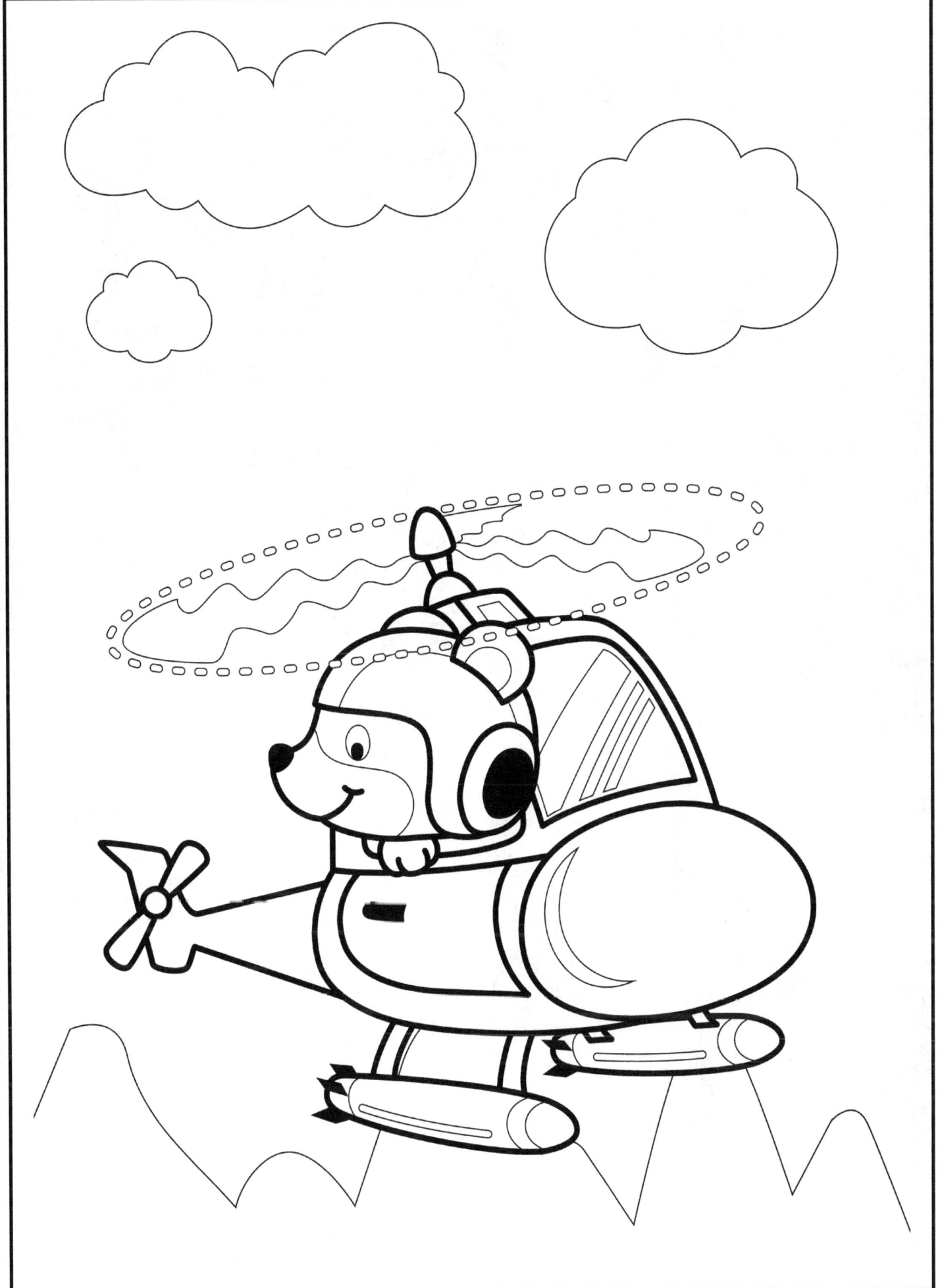

Dinosaur
COLORING BOOK

Includes Fun and Interesting Dinosaur Facts

DP KIDS PRESS

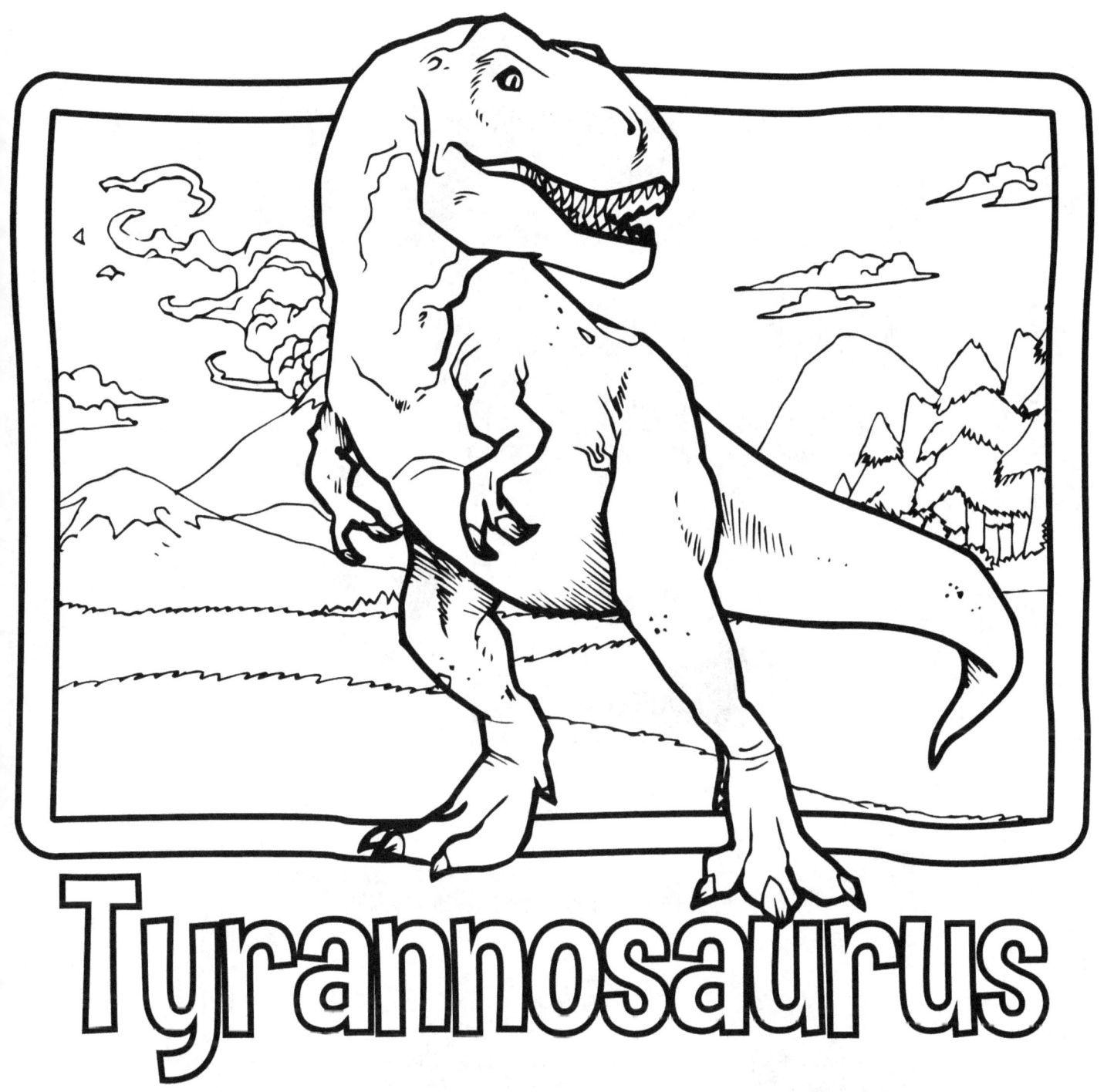

Tyrannosaurus

Tyrannosaurus Rex means "Tyrant Lizard." The T. Rex was up to 40 feet in length and could run up to 20 miles per hour. They lived during the late Cretaceous period.

THINGS THAT GO
VEHICLE
COLORING BOOK

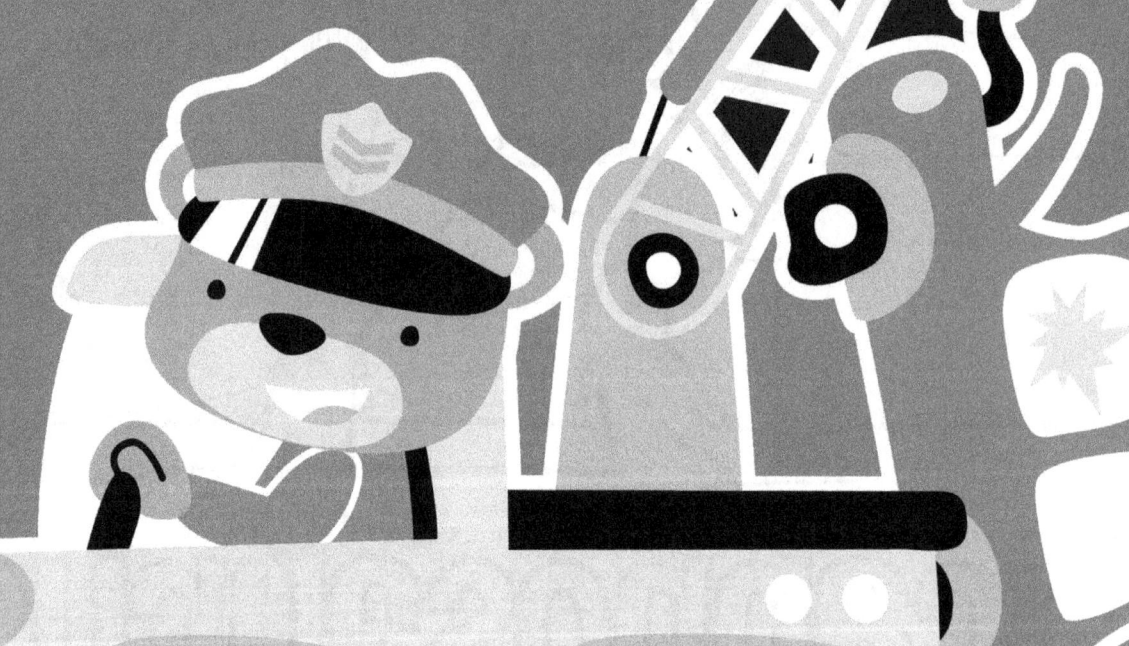
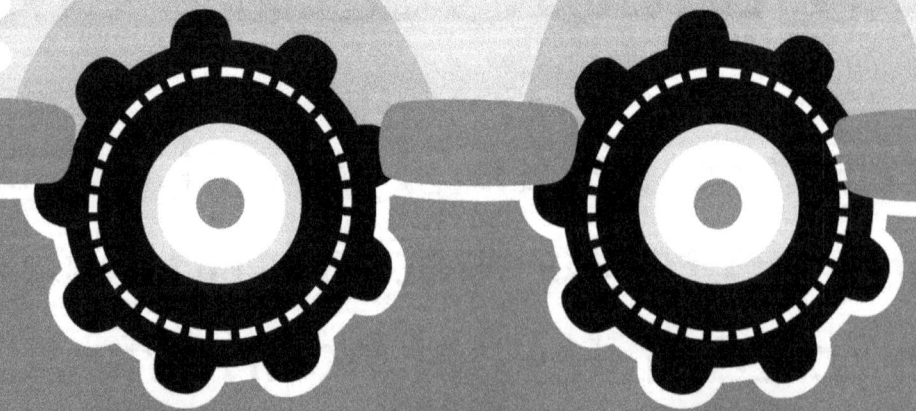

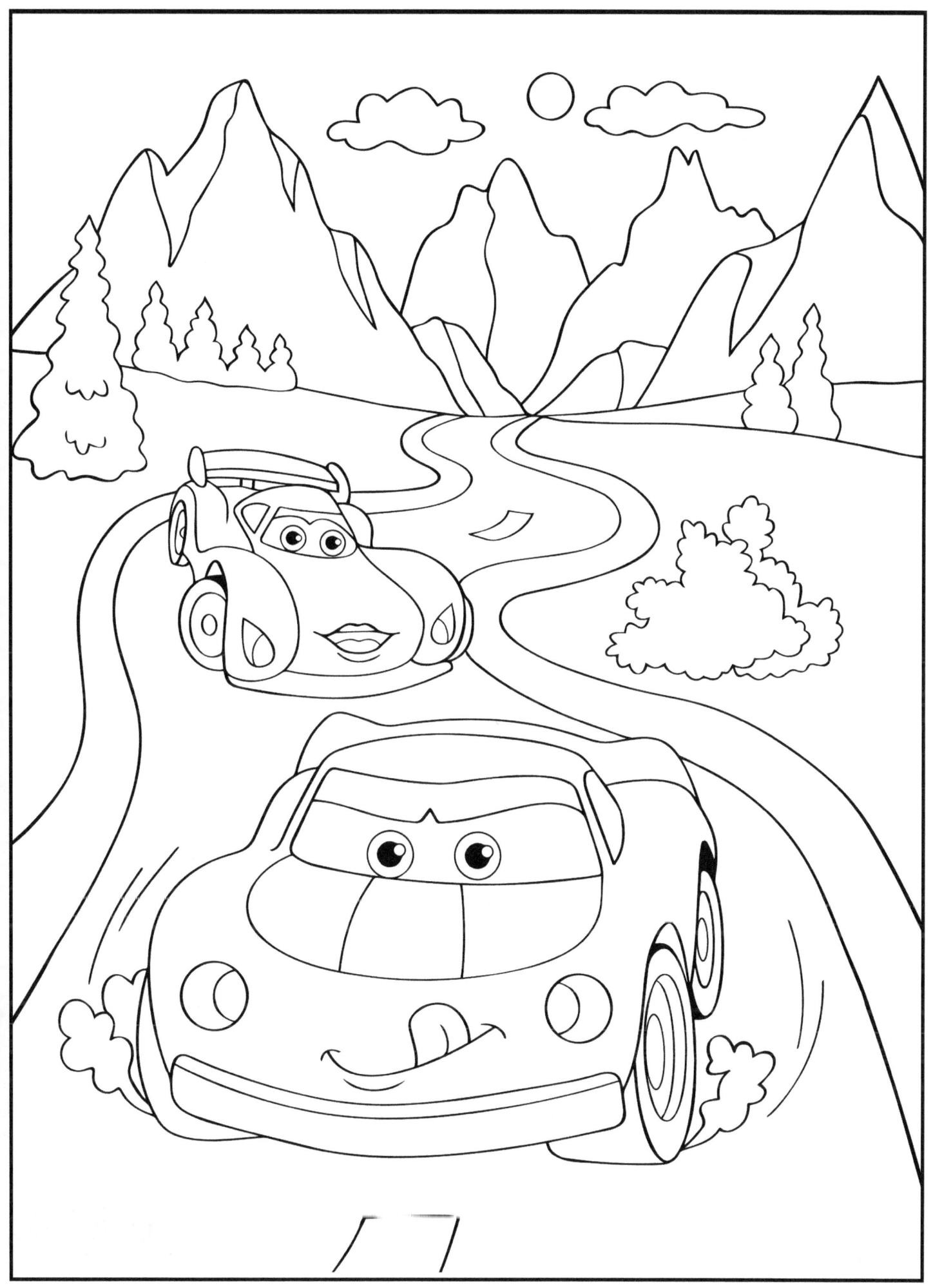

CPSIA information can be obtained
at www.ICGtesting.com
Printed in the USA
LVHW061811081219
639816LV00020B/96/P